The Smithsonian Book of Flight for Young People

An Italian Caproni Stipa, with "venturi-tube" fuselage.

Igor Sikorsky's Ilya Muromets *(1914), the first four-engine bomber.*

THE SMITHSONIAN BOOK OF

A U.S. Navy McDonnell Phantom II jet, shortly after launch.

ALADDIN BOOKS

MACMILLAN PUBLISHING COMPANY   NEW YORK

COLLIER MACMILLAN PUBLISHERS   LONDON

FLIGHT
FOR YOUNG PEOPLE

By WALTER J. BOYNE

Dedicated to
Paul Edward Garber
NASM Historian Emeritus

Aladdin Books
Macmillan Publishing Company
866 Third Avenue, New York, NY 10022
Collier Macmillan Canada, Inc.

First Aladdin Books edition 1988

Printed in the United States of America

Design by Lynn Braswell

A hard cover edition of The Smithsonian Book of Flight for
Young People *is available from Atheneum, Macmillan Publishing*
Company.

10   9   8   7   6   5   4   3   2   1

Library of Congress Cataloging-in-Publication Data
Boyne, Walter J.
The Smithsonian Book of Flight for Young People/by Walter J. Boyne.
   Summary: A history of human flight, from man's oldest dreams,
through the world wars, which generated rapid advances in aviation,
to the present jet age.
   1. Aeronautics—History—Juvenile literature. [1. Aeronautics—
History] I. Boyne, Walter J., 1929- II. Title.
TL547.K39   1988   G29.13'009   88-985
ISBN 0-689-71212-X

CONTENTS

The U.S. Navy's Blue Angels in their Douglas A-4s.

Part 1

Today the idea of flight is something that most of us take very much for granted. Every day hundreds of thousands of people board airplanes of every size and description and travel through the sky at heights and speeds that, until the turn of the century, few ever believed possible. Before the Wright brothers achieved the first manned flight in 1903, most people thought traveling through the air in a machine was an idea contrary to common sense: flight was for birds; if people were meant to get off the ground and into the air, they would have been born with wings. And yet, the fact that flight was one of mankind's dreams was the very thing that made the actuality possible. For even though people are born without wings, they are born with an ability to make their dreams come true.

It is only natural that people would dream of traveling above the earth and into the sky. From the beginnings of history, people have placed their deities in the sky. The ability to fly seems mysterious, superhuman, something that belongs to the gods alone. To achieve flight might enable mere mortals to commune with those gods—in a sense, to be more like them.

And so flight has always seemed an almost magical feat. Even though we live in an age in which space travel, robots, and men on the moon are facts of life, there is still an aura of mystery and awe surrounding man's travels into the sky. Although we now can easily explain how airplanes and even spacecraft work, there is still something about the sight of an enormous man-made machine aloft that makes us believe, again, in miracles.

Airborne in the 1901 glider, Wilbur Wright learns how to fly, an obvious skill that was often neglected by would-be inventors of the flying machines.

From Dream to Reality

MONTGOLFIER IN THE CLOUDS

CONSTRUCTING OF AIR BALLOONS FOR THE GRAND MONARQUE

O by gar! dis be de grande invention. — Dis will immortalize my King, my Country, and myself:
We will declare de War against our ennemi; we will make des English quake, by gar:
We will inspect their Camp, we will intercept their Fleet, and we will set fire to their Dock-yards:
And by gar, we will take de Gibraltar in de air balloon, and when we have
Conquered d'Eenglish, den we conquer d'other Countrie, and make them all Colonie
to de Grand Monarque.

FOURTH SKETCH

Published as the act directs March 2 1784 by S. Fores No 3 Piccadilly

a Companion to this in a few days

LIGHTER THAN AIR— HEAVIER THAN AIR

Nearly everyone knows of the famous flights taken by Wilbur and Orville Wright at Kitty Hawk, North Carolina, in 1903, but not so many realize that people had been experimenting with the idea of flying for hundreds of years before that. Human flight was one of the oldest dreams on earth and, until that cold day in December, one that had never quite been realized.

The materials that the Wright brothers used to make their first unpowered gliders, wood and fabric, had been available on earth for thousands of years. Technically, manned flight had been possible since the kite was invented in China or Southeast Asia, more than two thousand years prior to the flight at Kitty Hawk. As early as the fifteenth century, Leonardo da Vinci, the famous artist and inventor, dreamed of flying and made inspired sketches of flying machines, some even with propellers, or "airscrews." And indeed, attempts at manned flight using hang gliders, kites, and birdlike models have been recorded through the centuries. But it was the Wright brothers who brought the different approaches to flying together in the first real airplane, an invention that would change life on earth—and above it—forever.

Despite attempts to fly in all manner of gliders, manned propellers, and whatever other crude devices experimenters thought would take to the air, the most popular and most successful of the flight experiments that preceded

Joseph Montgolfier, one of two brothers who invented the hot-air balloon in France in 1783, appears in this British poster that ridicules Montgolfier's claim that he would use the balloon to revolutionize warfare and defeat the English.

the Wright brothers' made use of the balloon. The Wright brothers were the first to bring the concept of a light, aerodynamically designed craft together with a method of propulsion: an engine. Experimentation with balloon flight rested on a different principle. By coincidence, two other brothers, Joseph and Etienne Montgolfier, of France, were the first to achieve real success with a balloon. By June of 1783, the Montgolfier brothers had perfected the aerostat, a device designed on the simple principle that heat rises—and when heat or hot air can be contained, in a balloon, for example, it will cause the balloon to rise.

The Montgolfiers' aerostat consisted of a small, straw-fed fire that heated the air in a huge linen bag that was lined with paper. Once inflated, the bag expanded to more than 100 feet in circumference. Their big, open-air experiments attracted much attention, and before long the brothers were invited to make a presentation at France's esteemed Academy of Sciences.

Every good idea has competition, though, and in the case of the Montgolfier brothers, it came from a man named J.A.C. Charles. Charles believed that hydrogen, a gas weighing only one-fourteenth as much as air, would provide more lift than heated air, and on August 24, 1783, he displayed his hydrogen balloon before an enthusiastic crowd that included Benjamin Franklin.

Thus, in the same manner were born two technologies that are still in use today: the hot-air and hydrogen balloons. Born too was the idea of competition in flight technology. The

*An unidentified Parisian couple celebrates the
glory of flight from the gondola of their balloon.
The banners bear a Latin phrase that means
"Thus one goes to the stars."*

rivalry of the Montgolfiers and J.A.C. Charles created two ways of ballooning instead of one, each with its advantages and disadvantages, each making an important contribution to the science of flight.

Less than two months later, on October 15, 1783, the first manned balloon flight was undertaken by J. F. Pilatre de Rozier. Although it was a tethered flight (the balloon was secured by ropes on the ground), de Rozier soared to a height of more than 80 feet, and so took one of man's first giant steps into the sky.

A number of early balloonists immediately saw the possibilities for this new invention. Tethered balloons were useful for observation, and balloons were used by the French to escape besieged Paris during the Franco-Prussian War.

In America, the idea of balloon flight was not as popular as it might have been. During the nineteenth century, the new nation was preoccupied with its push westward. Settling the vast country in farms and cities took up much of the energy and attention that might otherwise have been shared by the new prospects in flight. Despite the relative lack of enthusiasm, some record-breaking flights were made in America, including one by John Wise, a veteran balloonist, who flew an astonishing 1,120 miles from St. Louis, Missouri, to Henderson, New York, in 1859, longer than any contemporary European flight.

But the balloons of these early experimenters had a major flaw: they had no steering mechanism, and both pilot and passenger were more or less at the mercy of ever-changing winds. Riding in an early balloon was very much like drifting in a boat without oars or motor: you could assume and even calculate that certain currents would carry the craft to your destination, but without a means of steering, there was no real guarantee that you would get where you wanted to go.

It wasn't until 1852 that a man named Henri Giffard developed the idea that would solve this initial problem of air navigation. In trying to devise means by which to steer and navigate, Giffard was the first to introduce machinery to the balloon, combining the two into something entirely new. His *dirigible* (a French word that means "steerable") was powered by a steam engine that drove three propellers, and a triangular rudder at the rear gave steering capability. Giffard's airship made its historic first flight from Paris to Trappes, France, on September 24, 1852, averaging about five miles per hour. Clearly, the invention of the dirigible was another great step forward in the history of flight.

But dirigibles were not without their problems, either. The steam engines used to power the vehicles were too heavy and slow for practical use. Internal-combustion engines, like those soon to be used in the development of automobiles, were far too dangerous for use near the highly flammable hydrogen that provided the dirigible's lift. One spark from the engine could set off a huge explosion! But despite the dangers, construction of dirigibles would continue for many years, and Giffard's introduction of the engine to the idea of flight

Energized by steam engines generating a total of 360 horsepower, Sir Hiram Maxim's tripleton biplane, left, almost flew in 1894. This version, with clipped wings, became a popular attraction at charity affairs.

caused many inventors and scientists to think about flight in an entirely new way.

While Giffard's dirigible used an engine for steering power and propulsion, it was still built on the "lighter-than-air" principle, using hydrogen gas for lift. But a new idea was slowly taking shape in the minds of flight enthusiasts. People began to puzzle over the idea that flight was possible in a "heavier-than-air" machine. A man named Sir George Cayley, a contemporary of Giffard's, was the first to explain the concept of heavier-than-air flight in mathematical terms. Cayley experimented with this principle on and off for nearly sixty years, and his work earned him the title of Father of Aeronautics. He was the first to understand that a vehicle of the proper weight, shape, and surface area could, with a sustained source of power, achieve flight.

Cayley's insights and experiments had their greatest influence not only in terms of their contribution to the creation of a successful airship, but also in the way in which Cayley's thinking encouraged other inventors and scien-

tists of his time. Cayley recorded and published most of his calculations and research and so was able to help other flight experimenters avoid his errors and incorporate his successes as they designed and constructed their own flying machines.

Although Cayley's ideas worked on paper, many experimenters misinterpreted them as they attempted to develop practical applications. Cayley's calculations had shown that heavier-than-air flight was possible, but many experimenters mistakenly believed that all they had to do to achieve flight was design the biggest and most powerful vehicle they could manage to construct, increasing Cayley's calculations arithmetically. None of them really worked. These huge machines ranged from the "Aerial Steam Carriage," granted a patent by the British government in 1843, to the steam-powered plane of Sir Hiram Maxim, the inventor of the machine gun.

Maxim's aircraft, named the *Leviathan*, was enormous. It had a wingspan of 104 feet, twin steam engines, each producing 180 horse-

Glider pioneer Otto Lilienthal, below, had a conical hill, right, built near Berlin. From the top, hang glider at the ready, he could leap into a breeze from any direction.

power, and weighed 3.5 tons. The *Leviathan* almost did succeed in becoming airborne, in a sense, in 1894 (within guardrails that Maxim had devised), but Maxim inexplicably withdrew from flight experiments after that. The world would have to wait for the turn of the century before true flight could be achieved.

It is perhaps just as well that those who thought bigger was better in their flying machines were denied any real success, because each of these huge machines, once airborne, would still have lacked one crucial element: control. Much like the early balloonists, these experimenters were so involved in getting aloft that they didn't give proper attention to how to control the aircraft once it was in the sky! But unlike the balloons, these new flying machines were heavy and could be very dangerous, both to an unskilled pilot and to those on the ground. Should those gigantic planes have gotten airborne and then crashed, the wreckage could have killed or injured many people and caused a great deal of damage.

Not all of Cayley's successors were so mis-guided, however. In 1890 a man named Otto Lilienthal took the next major step in the history of flight. His creation of what would come to be called a glider (in modern terms a hang glider) proved to have a direct influence on the career of the Wright brothers. The "bigger-is-better" flight experiments were proven failures by then, and so Lilienthal turned his attention back to nature's exemplars of flight: birds. His gliders were light and easy to maneuver, and followed as far as it was possible their natural models. "Skins" of cotton canvas were stretched over "bones" of light and flexible willow wands in an attempt to duplicate the qualities of birds' wings. Curiously enough, Otto Lilienthal also had a brother, Gustav, with whom he collaborated. Like the Montgolfier brothers before them and the Wrights afterward, the Lilienthal brothers worked as an experimental team. Aside from being brothers, though, the Lilienthals were similar to the Wrights in other ways. Each brother reinforced the other, and each pair made important critical observations about the

Left, Lilienthal's remarkable series of over 2,000 flights came to an end on August 9, 1896, when he broke his back in a crash. Right, close-up view of the Wright's 1903 aircraft combination engine area and "cockpit." The pilot lay beside the four-cylinder engine, which powered the propellers through a system of sprockets and chains.

flight of birds and how to apply the principles of bird flight to their flying machines. Each team also worked from the known to the unknown in a very cautious manner, taking risks only when they felt their knowledge of a previous step in the experimental process was secure.

The unpowered Lilienthal machines were composed almost entirely of materials that had existed on earth for centuries, natural materials in keeping with Lilienthal's observations of natural flight. Otto Lilienthal's actual gliding experiments followed more than twenty-five years of study. The first of these took place in 1891; in the next five years, he made more than two thousand short flights before, in 1896, he was fatally injured in a fall to the ground. Perhaps the greatest imperfection in the Lilienthal machines centered, again, on the problem of control. They depended on the pilot's shifting his weight to steer the vehicle, a method that does not provide the craft with any real guidance. The weight-shifting method of control presumes skill on the part of

the pilot, hard to come by in these early days of flight. Nevertheless, the Lilienthals' work advanced aviation further than anyone had before them. Otto Lilienthal provided a shining example to all flight experimenters who followed him. Not only was he an engineer, he was a real pilot. Lilienthal also wanted the world to know about his work: his feats of glider flight, brief successes as well as dismal failures, are carefully documented in photographs.

Like Lilienthal, the Wrights performed their first experiments in long glider flights that taught them how to fly. During those flights, they also learned that a positive method of control was superior to weight shifting. The Wright brothers became famous because they were the first to manage a successful manned flight of a heavier-than-air craft, but they were successful only because they were able to analyze and correct many of the causes of other experimenters' failures. Like all successful inventors, the Wrights saw mistakes not as failures, but as problems—problems that

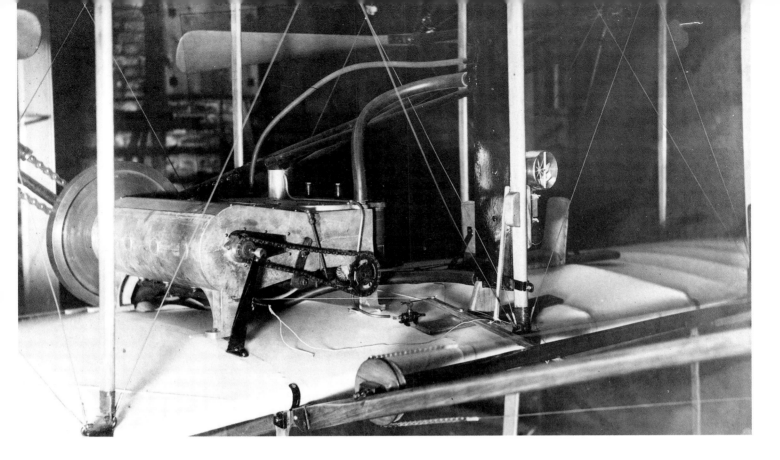

could, with time and patience, be solved.

Prior to becoming flight experimenters, the Wrights had been bicycle makers and mechanics. Bicycle technology would come to the rescue more than once in the Wrights' search for a successful airplane. Early on, they were able to take their knowledge of mechanics and create a wind tunnel at their bicycle factory. Inside the wind tunnel, they actually could see how air currents affected different configurations of wing structures, and so were able to design and build full-sized wings that would give their aircraft the lift and balance it needed. The Wrights also realized that a propeller was in fact a rotating wing.

It has been said that the Wright Flyer was a marriage of bicycle technology and a box-kite glider. All it needed was a source of power. And that power was delivered to the propeller from a lightweight, internal-combustion, gasoline engine of the Wrights' own design. The pilot lay on the lower wing next to the four-cylinder engine.

Though it all seems simple enough today, the Wright Flyer was the product of years of experimentation, calculation, and trial and error. Yet on December 17, 1903, this relatively simple machine was the first ever to achieve true manned and powered flight. The first flight was little more than 120 feet; the day's final flight came in at a time of only 59 seconds and a distance of 852 feet. Yet, as insignificant as it may sound to us now, that day at Kitty Hawk took the world a distance far greater than 852 feet.

Overleaf: In aviation's premier moment, Orville Wright makes the first successful takeoff in the Flyer on December 17, 1903. This 120-foot leap was surpassed by the day's final flight of 59 seconds and a distance of 852 feet. Inset: Wilbur and his mustachioed brother, Orville, at the windy site near Kitty Hawk, North Carolina, where much of their testing took place.

FROM FIRST TO LAST

The Wright brothers may have led the way to the sky, yet, over the next ten years, in the period just before the First World War, their remarkable feats soon fell far behind those of engineers and aviators in Europe. Ten years after the flight at Kitty Hawk, America, the country that had brought the world its first real airplanes, ranked well behind the leading European countries in production and design of practical aircraft.

How did this happen? Part of the problem involved the Wrights themselves. The brothers were not the kind of men who were cut out for celebrity status; they were far too serious and shy to demand the attention that their Flyer deserved. In fact, their flights at Kitty Hawk had not been witnessed by the public. Keep in mind, too, that flight was still something that few people believed was possible until they saw it with their own eyes. In many parts of America, flying machines were still considered flukes, carnival tricks that few people could take seriously. That attitude also helps to explain the Wright brothers' reluctance to share their discoveries. Nevertheless, it was a problem that truly hampered the continued development of aviation in this country. The Wright brothers' reluctance to share their discoveries also grew out of their strong objections to competition.

One of the best known of their competitors was Glenn Curtiss, who became involved in

European enthusiasm for flight soared after Wilbur Wright's exhibitions in 1908. Soon developments in the Old World outdistanced those in America, as might be suggested by this jubilant 1909 poster for a flying meet in Reims, France.

lengthy patent battles with them over the years. Like the Wrights, Curtiss had been a bicycle mechanic. Subsequently he became involved with motorcycles, and was well-known as a record-setting motorcycle racer and as an inventor of powerful, lightweight engines. After Wilbur Wright's successful flight at Kitty Hawk, it didn't take Curtiss long to figure out that his engines could be useful in flying machines. For a while, Curtiss had no personal involvement in aviation. As early as 1906 he did offer to sell his engines to the Wrights, but by then the Wrights had made some improvements of their own and weren't interested in outside help. During the three years following the Kitty Hawk flight, the Wrights had made many improvements on the original Flyer and had taken out patents on everything that pertained to the design of their flying machines. Furthermore, they made no secret of the fact that they were fully prepared to challenge in court anyone who infringed on those patents in conducting experiments. It is hard to know what motivated the Wright brothers in this instance. Perhaps they were only trying, and rightfully so, to protect their work. Or perhaps this attitude was simply in keeping with everything that we know of them as men. They were careful people who wanted to take the necessary time to experiment and improve the Flyer on their own terms without having to worry about competition from other inventors. At any rate, the Wrights did what they could to squelch competition in the air, and this strategy hampered improvement and development of aircraft in America.

With engine and engineering knowledge honed by his experience
in motorcycle manufacturing, Glenn Curtiss made his way
into the field of aviation, eventually working with Alexander
Graham Bell on his own early bid for flight.

Other aviation experimenters were frustrated by the Wrights' continuing close-to-the-chest policy about their inventions and their refusal to share what they knew with others in the field. Nonetheless, experimentation did continue. Eventually, Glenn Curtiss hooked up with another great thinker of his time, Alexander Graham Bell, the inventor of the telephone and, along with a few other dedicated aviation enthusiasts, founded a company in Canada called the Aerial Experiment Association (AEA). When Curtiss joined this group he brought to it more than his knowledge of mechanics. He had competed in races and in business; he knew the value of team effort and of getting public attention for his accomplishments. Together, the AEA team created a series of aircraft called "Dromes" (short for aerodromes). Drome No. 1 was called the *Red Wing*, Drome No. 2 the *White Wing*. Both taught the group how to build an airplane and fly it for seconds at a time. Then in 1908, Drome No. 3, the *June Bug*, catapulted the AEA and Glenn Curtiss into the world's spotlight.

The date was July 4, 1908; the place, Hammondsport, New York. In addition to a huge holiday crowd, a motion-picture camera crew and a bevy of newspaper reporters and photographers were present to capture the event. Keep in mind that until this point, the Wright brothers had never flown at a public event. With the flight of the *June Bug*, Curtiss would attempt to capture the prizes offered by *Scientific American* and the New York Aero Club for one simple feat: to fly on schedule, on a given date and from a specified location, for a distance of more than one kilometer.

In those early days of aviation, a flight of such distance seemed almost too daring to be conceivable. The tension of the crowd increased as wind and rain delayed the *June Bug*'s takeoff for many hours. It wasn't until almost six in the evening that the *June Bug* was rolled out and its engines started up. By seven o'clock the weather had cleared enough, and Curtiss did fly, but fell short of the one-kilometer goal. Half an hour later, he tried again—and with yellow wings waggling, smoke pouring from the 40-horsepower Curtiss engine, hands clenching the steering mechanism in a death grip, Curtiss flew. At a height of about 20 feet, the *June Bug* flew for more than a mile. In a single stroke, Curtiss had captured not only the coveted *Scientific American* prize, but also $12,500 in prize money. Curtiss knew now that he was totally committed to aviation. And perhaps more important, the world knew, for the first time, that the airplane had actually been invented! Flight—real flight—was not only possible; it had happened. It was something that hundreds of people had seen with their own eyes and thousands more had seen documented in newspapers and in moving pictures!

Curtiss's flight had enormous impact, not only in making Curtiss and the AEA famous, but on the Wright brothers as well. For the first time, the Wrights realized that they had some genuine competition—competition from which even their many patents could not entirely protect them. Their patent battles had a

With June Bug, *Glenn Curtiss flew a kilometer course non-stop and won a prize offered by* Scientific American *magazine in 1908. Although the resulting publicity thrust Curtiss into the limelight,* June Bug *was hardly controllable as an aircraft, a problem that the Wrights had long since solved.*

suffocating effect on manufacture up to that point, but now it was clear that there were other aspects of competition beyond patents: public acclaim, for one. The Wrights had been negotiating for some time with the United States government for a contract to produce military aircraft, but were asking $100,000 per plane. After Curtiss's flight, they began to negotiate more reasonably, and brought the price down to $25,000 each. But they knew that ties with the military were not all they needed to maintain their supremacy in the field of aviation. They needed, as Curtiss already knew, the enthusiasm of the general public—whether they wanted it or not!

Wilbur set his sights on Europe, perhaps in an attempt to bring flight to worldwide attention, rather than choosing to compete with Curtiss and the AEA for national recognition. The Wrights had shipped a plane to France in 1907 but had been unable to make suitable arrangements for a demonstration flight. Now, in the summer of 1908, Wilbur traveled to France and on August 8 began a series of flights near Le Mans that astounded the Europeans. He demonstrated to the Continental audience what seemed to be an absolute mastery of the air and they threw themselves at his feet. But these demonstrations had a curious side effect that Wilbur may not have counted on. He so awed his audiences that almost immediately a host of European competitors leapt into action. Some of the same people who witnessed the flights of Wilbur Wright that summer in Europe would go on to make such incredible advances in aviation over the

Wilbur Wright conquers Europe from the air as his Flyer appears at a French airfield, where coachmen steady their startled horses as the Flyer clamors overhead.

next five years that the Wright Flyer, and indeed all the other American aircraft, would very soon be rendered hopelessly obsolete—dinosaurs in the very field they had created.

Back home, the Wright brothers brought suit against Curtiss and the AEA for patent infringement, creating a court battle that would drag on for many years. The fact that the Wrights were willing to challenge their competitors in court continued to have a dampening effect on American aviation. Perhaps they had moral and legal grounds for such lawsuits, but in pursuing them, they neglected the idea of aviation as a national goal rather than a private enterprise. Building the world's greatest airplanes would place the United States in a position of unqualified strength. That was not yet to be.

These were the years just prior to World War I. Political trouble and the possibility of war loomed all over Europe, but the pervading American mood was that of isolationism, a kind of "you mind your business and I'll mind mine" attitude. Many Americans believed that Europe's political problems were just that—Europe's problems—and they wanted them to stay that way. Americans did not want to participate in world politics. No one suspected that America would eventually become involved in World War I, nor did anyone foresee the value of the airplane in the conflict to come. So aviation in America was stifled not only in the private sector where patent battles raged, but also in the military, which might have provided the boost American aviation needed. For the next few years, American

flight remained a sideshow entertainment, the domain of daredevils and entrepreneurs. And the American pilots who emerged in those early years fit that mold quite nicely.

Manned flight had a profoundly different effect on the minds and the hearts of Europeans. They were more aware of the possibilities of war. Intricate political alliances arose among the various nations as tensions grew. With war on their minds, the French immediately saw the military advantages of the airplane, and England, Germany, and Russia soon did too.

Besides the complex political atmosphere, though, there was another important factor separating the American and European attitudes toward flying machines. Unlike the American impression of flying as a sideshow featuring foolhardy but awesome daredevils, flight held a different sort of fascination for the European aristocracy: it became a sport of the rich and famous. At the Le Mans racetrack, some of the car tracks were converted to aviation fields. Soon, airplane races gained as much appeal as car races, a fact that contributed to the technological advance of early European flight. As with cars, the aristocrats were willing to spend money on the development of winning machines! To win a race, a plane had to be fast and well-controlled. And the Europeans built those planes. France soon took the lead in prewar aviation, with advancements by such men as Louis Blériot, whose tiny plane made the first successful crossing of the English Channel on July 25, 1909.

Among the aristocracy, there was also a mil-

itary element. Sons of noble European families routinely went into military service. An officer of noble blood, newly fascinated with aviation, could influence his government to appropriate funds for the development of military flying machines. From 1908 until the outbreak of World War I, Germany is reputed to have spent $73 million on aviation, France almost $35 million, and Russia $34 million. In the United States, only $685 thousand was spent during the same period. Our refusal to invest in aircraft development, perhaps more than anything else, led to the rapid decline of America's brief leadership in the field.

In 1908 Wilbur Wright held the distance, altitude, duration, and speed records docu-

mented by the Fédération Aéronautique Internationale. In the years that followed, those records were broken once, and sometimes twice, every year. By 1911 American aircraft were no longer capable of competing in races against the new European aircraft. In that same year, the first major long-distance air race started in Paris, ran across France,

France's lead in pre-World War I aviation is evidenced by their homegrown hero—Louis Blériot—who flew across the English Channel on July 25, 1909. Opposite, his tiny plane takes off from Calais, France. Above, tumultuous Londoners greet the French aviator after his daring feat.

Belgium, and Holland, over the English Channel to London, and back to Paris. Of the forty-three entrants, flying twelve different kinds of planes, there was only one American—in a French plane! Only nineteen contestants ever made it through the first leg of the journey, and only nine crossed the finish line. Three other pilots were killed in the course of that fateful race and six were badly injured. Although air travel had made many incredible advances, it was far from safe.

Despite the lid on spending and development in the United States, aviation struggled on, primarily on the sideshow and exhibition circuit. Though America wasn't making much of a contribution to the technological side of aviation in those years, it was making a contribution to the personal history of flight. Our daredevil approach to piloting aircraft was producing some of the most colorful and dashing

men and women America had ever seen. Yet, early pilots such as Charles Hamilton or Lincoln Beachey were viewed in much the same way as Harry Houdini—as great magicians who weren't afraid to risk their lives. The list of those early pilots, each of whose feats was more daring than the last, is long and impressive. Stunt flying became the real show and these pilots were ready to perform.

Lincoln Beachey was perhaps the premier pilot of that era. Beachey began his career at the age of eighteen. Before long, he was hired as a test pilot for Glenn Curtiss. Time passed and Beachey went out on his own, establishing a repertoire of spirals, dives, and stunts that would make him famous. When Beachey learned that Edouard Pégoud, a European pilot, had performed a death-defying loop in 1913, Beachey immediately commissioned his old boss, Curtiss, to design a specially rein-

Opposite, a close-up of the fragile aircraft that carried Louis Blériot across the English Channel. Cold, tired, and angry, Jules Vérdrines, right, won the Paris to Madrid race in 1911. The only pilot to finish, he was, nonetheless, later than expected and the crowds had gone home.

forced biplane—a "heavy looper"—for him. The first plane crashed, but the next one was successful and Beachey used it to perform an ever-increasing number of breathtaking loops, dizzying spirals, and long, long dives. New stunts demanded new airplanes, and Beachey got them. One of these stunt craft, *The Little Looper*, was a biplane with an 80-horsepower engine. Small and powerful, it was so successful that Beachey commissioned designer Warren Eaton for an even more radical stunt craft.

A modern-looking affair with a wingspan of 26 feet and tricycle landing gear, this even littler looper achieved a top speed of 104 miles per hour. On March 14, 1915, Beachey made his last flight. Taking off from San Francisco's Panama Pacific International Exposition Grounds on a bright Sunday afternoon, Beachey climbed out over the bay toward Al-

catraz. Reversing course, he headed into a series of loops, losing altitude with each one. After leveling off and then climbing to an altitude of 3,500 feet, he dove straight down, finally pushing past the vertical so the crowd could read "BEACHEY" spelled out on the wings. At a sizzling 180 miles per hour, he pulled sharply on the stick to regain level flight, but his wings broke away. Though he survived the initial crash into the bay, the daredevil was trapped inside the wreckage and drowned.

It was this era of daredevils that saw the first women to enter the world of flight. Harriet Quimby, America's first woman to pilot a plane, unfortunately would lose her life in a freak accident. She and a friend, equipped with neither seat belts nor parachutes, fell to their deaths when gusts of wind upturned the airplane. The airplane, however, landed safely.

COMPLIMENTS OF
MISS HARRIET QUIMBY

The luck of Harriet Quimby, above, America's first woman aviator, ran out when she and a friend fell to their deaths after gusts of wind up-turned their airplane. They had neither seatbelts nor parachutes, but the plane, ironically, landed safely.

Italian aircraft designer Giovanni Caproni in 1911 developed the Ca.9, opposite. The fine wooden monoplane was advanced for its day but suffered from an unreliable, three-cylinder radial engine.

Another, less typical daredevil hero was Charles Willard, a Harvard graduate and race-car driver. At the age of twenty-six, Willard was taught to fly by Glenn Curtiss. In August 1909, Willard, in the Curtiss *Golden Flyer*, broke the ten-mile distance record established by Orville Wright and Lt. Benjamin Foulois, the first U.S. Army airplane pilot. After completing a twelve-mile circuit over Long Island, Willard began to be called the Wizard of the Air. Within months his aerial feats brought him $1,000 per flight and $7,500 for a ten-day air meet.

Exhibition flyers could make a good deal of money in those early days, and Willard was one who used the nest egg he acquired to good advantage. Unfortunately, many of the daredevil flyers of the time simply didn't live long enough to go on to other things. A saying was common in early aviation: "There are plenty of bold flyers and plenty of old flyers, but hardly any old, bold flyers." But Willard beat the odds on both counts. He went on to establish a number of firsts in the course of his long and distinguished career. He worked on the first ground-to-air radio telephones and helped to develop the arresting gear used by Eugene Ely in the famous first landing on the deck of a ship. Willard was also the first pilot ever to be shot down—an irate farmer near Joplin, Missouri, put a bullet through his propeller! Sadly, though, Willard was by far not the last pilot to be shot down. For with the advent of World War I, when the airplane would truly come into its own, many more brave heroes, patriots, and daredevils in the skies would lose their lives.

Part 2

*The sound was entirely foreign to me. Faint, yet
permeating, it wavered into every room of our
sunny, country house—a hum without an apparent
source. I had been dutifully picking up toys, but the
sound had a strange urgency that drove all honorable
intention from my five-year-old mind.*

*"It's an aeroplane!" shouted one of my older
brothers, pronouncing the word as carefully as it
was spelled in those days. And we erupted from the
house, my parents, my sister, two brothers, and
myself, darting outside to stare. It came over the
pine trees, a thousand feet high, yellow wings and
dark fuselage startlingly clear against the clean New
England sky of 1922.*

*We gathered in a little knot, drawn together by
our wonder. Someone's hands were on my shoulders
as we looked up. By then a bit of the astonishment
had worn off for my elders, but it was totally new
to me, the youngest. I gazed at the airplane's steady
flight and savored its great noise—the thunder of
mighty cylinders, the slap of wooden propeller
blades, the cry of the air riven by struts and wires.
It wasn't really a strange new god, just a Curtiss
Jenny. But it gathered disciples. Of the four of us
siblings, standing there with Mother and Dad, two
became pilots and another married one.*

Edwards Park,
A Founding Editor, Smithsonian *magazine*

*In 1924, California flier Earl Daugherty steers a
Curtiss JN-4 Jenny while his partner, Auggy
Redlax, grabs for a cap.*

WORLD WAR I: THE ACCELERATOR

When the First World War began in August of 1914, neither the Allies (which included Britain, France, Russia, Italy, Japan, and the United States) nor the opposing alliance (including the Austro-Hungarian Empire, Germany, and Turkey) could be said to truly understand that the airplane had the power to permanently change the very nature of war. Aviation was still so new that the potential of the airplane as a weapon of war was just emerging. No one could yet foresee how crucial a role it would play as the conflict unfolded.

One of the most important functions the airplane would serve was in observation and in the gathering of information from aloft. Land-based military conflicts had always been fought over a portion of ground, with armies confronting each other directly in combat.

The past meets the future here, as British General Sir Horace Smith-Dorrien and his staff salute a B.E.2 biplane during an air review in May 1913. By the following year, military interest in the use of aircraft for reconnaissance prompted many European countries to experiment with aviation as a new tool for the military. Below, the Imperial and Royal Austro-Hungarian Field Pilot's badge of 1913—an early flight medal.

Early in World War I, both British (below) and German (opposite) recruiting posters lured volunteers with images of brave knights battling evil dragons. As the war progressed, however, the horrors of trench warfare made such storybook images difficult to believe. In search of glamour, eyes turned upward to the dashing aces who fought dogfights high above the bloody mud of the trenches.

BRITAIN · NEEDS

YOU · AT · ONCE

PUBLISHED BY THE PARLIAMENTARY RECRUITING COMMITTEE, LONDON.   POSTER Nº 108.   PRINTED BY SPOTTISWOODE & Cº Lᵀᴰ LONDON. E.C.

During World War I, the invention of the machine gun by Hiram Maxim and the use of massed artillery gave rise to what is called trench warfare, with each side hidden in long, deep ditches during battle. Once a portion of land was captured, new trenches were dug and the battle went on, sometimes for months, until the exhausted armies reached another entrenched stalemate. In order for a battle to be fought and won, it was essential for a commanding officer to find out as much as he could about what the other side was doing, their location, strategy, and so on. For this reason, armies needed scouts.

With machine guns protecting the opposing trenches, more traditional forms of military scouting such as runners and cavalry were soon rendered impractical: scouts would be shot before they could even get close. An aerial scout, however, could fly over the opposing army at a much safer distance and get a much broader view of what was going on. For the first time it was possible to see what was happening on "the other side of the hill," to know, or at least make an educated guess about, the opposing army's number of forces, artillery capability, and plans of attack.

Initially then, airplanes came into World War I solely for scouting. Or, to use more technical terms, for reconnaissance and surveillance. By 1915, aerial reconnaissance, both by eye and by camera, had reached very sophisticated levels. All of the maps for the famous Battle of Neuve-Chapelle, which began in France in March of that year, were based on aerial photos.

If the principal work of aircraft in the early years of the war was to gather information, an equally important task was to prevent the other side from being able to do the same thing. And prevention required aircraft that were armed. In those early days, armed aircraft were called pursuits. Today, we call them fighters. Pursuit attacks were in turn foiled by other pursuits. Thus a new battleground was established as the conflict between nations took to the skies. Though the war had started with unarmed aircraft—most often observation two-seaters like the French Voisins and Farmans—by the war's end, a whole new kind of airplane had developed: a single-seater fighting machine, designed only for war. Almost simultaneously with the development of the fighter plane, a third important type of combat aircraft began to emerge: the bomber. The earliest bombardiers were nothing more than a pilot or copilot dropping hand grenades or small bombs by hand from the cockpit! But as new as airplanes were to war, armies learned to use them very quickly. And that recognition of their utility gave rise to a need for more planes, better planes, and efficient technological support for this newest means of waging battle.

At the outset of the war, all of these developments were still very far from obvious. Military planners had an idea of what the airplane could mean to war, but putting that idea into efficient operation was not always simple. These were days when airplane designs were vastly different from one another. There were no such things as interchangeable parts or

Aiming by eye, a British bombardier of early World War I prepares to drop a bomb, by hand, on infantry below.

"standard" features. And the planes that came into the conflict at the war's beginning were, to say the least, a mixed bag. Sources reporting the numbers of aircraft available for combat duty in 1914 (the first year of the war) vary widely—mostly because it was difficult, in the early days of the conflict, to define exactly what a combat aircraft was. Most agree, however, that the Germans had about 450, a little more than half of which were ready for combat duty, as well as 11 dirigible airships. The French could fly about 300 aircraft, from a total of about 600, and a dozen dirigibles. And the British, at home and in France, had only about 160 craft, of which perhaps a third were of front-line quality. Part of the reason that so few of the aircraft could actually be used was

the huge variety available. The lack of consistency in design, engine capability, and the like created a whole new set of problems. With so many different types of planes flying under the hazardous conditions of combat, it was almost impossible to keep an airplane in good working order for any length of time. Parts for planes and even mechanics were very scarce. Once a plane was damaged it might be weeks or even months before it could be fixed and returned to active duty. The sheer variety of planes on duty during World War I was one factor, among others, that would have a great influence on the development of later military planes.

Still, the armies and their suppliers were learning more about the airplane and its capabilities all the time. They learned that better climb meant higher altitude and therefore more speed in a dive, and they tuned what aircraft they had accordingly. There came an increasing demand for new machines: more reliable planes with greater agility. It wasn't long before all armies realized that the aircraft in the field required, in addition to trained pilots, an enormous support system, including not only factories and skilled technicians, but also the industries and people that produced the raw materials necessary to make airplanes: high-quality wood, steel, copper, brass, and linen. Orders for planes and the materials needed to make them poured in from the fighting fronts in unimaginable numbers, and airplane production began to become a very important part of every fighting nation's total war effort.

The German Zeppelin Staaken VGO III, below, was the largest of all World War I bombers. It had a wingspan of 140 feet—just three feet shorter than the wingspan of the World War II B-29. The seven-man crew included a mechanic and pilots who struggled at the unwieldy controls of the giant plane. Bottom, grooves on the armored wedges bolted to the propeller of Jean Navarre's Morane-Saulnier N monoplane allowed the ace to shoot his machine gun, with relative safety, through the spinning propeller.

As we have seen, the use of airplanes for reconnaissance spawned the need for airplanes for pursuit. The first real step toward the development of pursuit, or fighter, planes came in March of 1915 when a French pilot named Roland Garros arranged for some bullet deflection devices invented by another Frenchman, Raymond Saulnier, to be attached to the propeller blades of a Morane-Saulnier Type N. Early in the war, attempts to mount machine guns on airplanes had been unsuccessful because of the extra weight they added. The Type N was a monoplane with a rotary engine of 110 horsepower and a top speed of 103 miles per hour at 6,500 feet. The performance was still not remarkable, but the bullet deflection devices, when attached to the propeller blades of Garros's plane, did permit him to fire a machine gun through the arc or "disk" formed by the whirling prop without shooting off the blades.

A gun mounted this way made it easier for the pilot to hit another airplane. Garros could aim his whole plane and pull the trigger. The effect was revolutionary. Garros shot down a German two-seater on April 1, 1915, with two more to follow that same month. But on April 19, a single German rifle bullet cut Garros's gas line and he was forced to land. Garros was unable to destroy the aircraft before the Germans discovered the design and position of his deflector shields—the Allies' secret was out.

But German efforts to develop similar shields did not meet with quite the same success. It seemed that copying the design of Garros's shields was easy; getting them to work was not. Whether the Germans simply used inferior metal in their shields or German bullets were simply better at piercing the metal is not known, but in the German experiments with the deflector shields the gun simply shot the propeller off. Frustrated, they called in a young Dutch designer, a man named Anthony Fokker, to help with the problem.

Fokker was a real genius whose reputation was often damaged by his own bragging and by problems with quality control in the aircraft he designed. When he was confronted with the German problem of developing armed pursuit planes, Fokker immediately rejected the whole idea of deflector shields and instead turned his team to the development of a synchronizing system. Mounted on a plane

of his own design, the Fokker M 5K monoplane, the machine-gun fire was momentarily interrupted whenever the propeller blades were in front of the muzzle of the gun; therefore, no bullets would hit the blades.

Fokker's plane itself was very small, with a wingspan of only about 28 feet, and its top speed was about 82 miles per hour. Nevertheless, armed with its synchronizing system, it did the job. The Allies would eventually develop their own synchronizing system, but for the time being at least, the Germans had the advantage in the skies. The Germans immediately ordered fifty of the planes, to be known as Eindeckers, built and parceled out to various squadrons. Before long the Eindeckers, in the hands of pilots such as Max Immelman, began to be known as the "Fokker Scourge," winning for their pilots many wartime decorations, such as the "Blue Max," as the German "Pour le Merite" medal was called, and vastly affected the air war on the western front.

Opposition to the Fokkers was light at first. The British were flying slow and relatively stable B.E.2cs and Maurice Farman "box kites" and initially sought some protection against the German threat through formation flying. The French tried to counter with Blériots and Nieuport 11s (nicknamed Bébés). None except the Nieuport was particularly effective against the superior German planes and ammunition. The Fokkers continued to stalk the front.

Another reason the German air war was so successful at this time was that the Germans

Right, three men who represented German aerial prowess during World War I: from the left, Bruno Loerzer, an expert flier-fighter; Anthony Fokker, the highly successful Dutch designer of war machines; and Hermann Goering, the leader after the death of Manfred von Richthofen (the Red Baron) of Germany's most feared pursuit squadron. Goering later played a pivotal role in Germany's Third Reich during World War II.

Germany's air superiority during early 1916 was partially a result of the development of the interrupter gear, left, by Anthony Fokker, which synchronized machine-gun fire with the spinning propeller, enabling German aviators to fire directly ahead with greater accuracy. Overleaf: an artists' rendering of a stricken German aircraft and a clear victory for the French Nieuport 11, high above the clouds.

Manfred Freiherr von Richthofen—the infamous Red Baron, center—with the squadron he led. Above, a German World War I aviator's medal.

were the first to learn the value of systematic deployment of aircraft units. Specific types of planes were grouped with the right pilots, trainers, and mechanics and sent to the area where they would be most useful. The best and most efficient planes were sent to the fronts where the action was hottest. Thus, the Germans were able to overcome, to some extent, the problems of inconsistency in design and shortages of parts and supplies. By the end of 1915, they had deployed more than eighty individual divisions of aircraft, including the first specially designated bombing squadrons.

But at about the same time, an Englishman, Captain Geoffrey de Havilland, designed the D.H.2. The D.H.2 was capable of 90 miles an hour and was highly maneuverable. Armed with a Lewis machine gun that was mounted directly in front of the pilot, while the propeller was in the rear, the D.H.2 soon proved

itself to be the Fokker's master. The British soon began an all-out offensive to drive the Germans back to their own soil; that, coupled with French efforts, brought the brief period of German air superiority to an end. In June of 1916, with the death of Max Immelman, the Germans were on the losing side, at least in the air.

There followed in Germany a shake-up in the high command. Fokkers no longer ruled the skies over the front, and the Germans were quick to recognize the need for improved aircraft. Control of the army and state was turned over to Field Marshal Paul von Hindenberg and General Erich Ludendorff, who wasted no time in calling for a new program of aircraft production. The Fokker designs had become outdated in less than a year. In desperation, the high command called for copies of French Nieuports to go into production. And as was frequently the case, the German copies turned out to be superior to the original.

Called the Albatros D I and designed by Robert Thelen, this German version had one major advantage over other fighters of its time: dual Spandau machine guns mounted near the cockpit. With double the firepower, the tide could again turn to the German side. Oswald Boelcke, another hero of the German air war, began an intense training program for his men, carefully drilling them before launching the new pilots, called "cubs," into combat in the fall of 1916. In the hands of Boelcke's students, among them the truly legendary Manfred von Richthofen, who was later dubbed the "Red Baron," the Albatros dominated the German Air Service through the summer of 1918.

It was with the Albatros that the Germans, spearheaded by von Richthofen, began the 1917 aerial campaign known as "Bloody April." Sitting behind two reliable machine guns, these pilots were able to establish—for the last time—German air superiority in the war. The Germans concentrated first on the British after the French temporarily withdrew much of their air force for a refitting after the famous Battle of Verdun. The Germans fought so fiercely and inflicted so many casualties on the British that the life expectancy for a pilot of the Royal Flying Corps was officially calculated at 17.5 hours! In that offensive, the British lost 151 planes, the Germans only 51.

To draw British fighters away from the front, the Germans planned a bombing offensive known as the Gotha raids. The initial attack over Folkestone, England, by 21 twin-engine Gotha bombers left 95 dead and 195 wounded. The British were shocked. Bombing had been taking place, off and on, ever since the beginning of the war, but this was different. The Gothas had flown in formation—in broad daylight—and their raid had resulted in the death of civilians and destruction of private property. This was no longer a war between armies: with the advent of bombing raids it became everyone's war. The raids continued and on June 13, 1917, bombs fell over London, killing 162 and injuring 438. Something had to be done. Almost immediately, the Britons responded with some important advances in technology: an efficient aircraft reporting system, aircraft detection devices, searchlights, and night fighters, all of which would contribute to Britain's success in driving off the German attacks.

Nineteen seventeen was also important because that was the year the United States first entered the war. Although the United States had lagged far behind Europe in military aircraft development, when she finally joined the Allies, America's enormous natural resources provided the means for massive production of military planes and parts. It was with American involvement that true standardization of aircraft, including interchangeable parts, came into being. In a little less than a year, the United States trained tens of thousands of workers in airplane manufacture. By the end of the war in 1918, America was producing twelve thousand planes a year, and more important, thousands of pilots.

Leergewicht: 274
Nutzlast: 123
zul. Gesamtgewicht: 3975

Auf rechter Seite

Opposite, protected by a nose gunner who, with two other crew members, breathed oxygen from tubes during high-altitude bombing missions, Germany's Gotha G V bombers brought a new dimension of destruction to World War I. Their raid in June 1917 caused 600 British casualties—including many civilians—and the destruction of private property.

After the first American pilots made their debut in the skies over Europe, German air superiority again began to slip. The Allies were quick to respond to the introduction of the Albatros with new tactics and better airplanes. Schools for "special flying" were established in Britain; here veteran pilots would pass on the facts of life and death to new recruits. And in the fall of 1917 came the plane that would put triumph in the skies back into the hands of the Allies: the British Sopwith Camel.

Though the Camels were dangerous to fly, these planes would kill more Germans than any other airplane. Despite the danger, those who piloted the original Sopwith Camels agree that it was an excellent fighter, fast and maneuverable. Other improved planes included the Bristol fighter and the great French SPAD XIII. Referred to as a "flying brick" by some pilots, the SPAD was a solid and powerful fighter plane, equipped with air-cooled machine guns.

But the war in the skies wasn't over yet, and the Germans again called upon Anthony Fokker for help and, while he could not be said to produce aircraft that were clearly superior to the Allies' Sopwiths and SPADs, he did produce two types of planes that kept the Germans competitive in the air war.

One of these was the Dr 1 Triplane, first introduced in 1917. Every bit as agile as the Sopwith Camel, the Fokker Triplane first arrived in relatively small numbers—only about 170—and stayed in use only for about a year. Though it had some quality control and struc-

Fearing meager volunteer turnout for the Air Service, the U.S. War department distributed patriotic posters, like the one above, and promised high rank. Fears proved groundless: the Air Service was flooded with eager applicants for flight training.

tural problems, it reinstated Fokker as a designer and paved the way for him to develop one of the most important planes of the war: the Fokker D VII, an airplane that would set the standard for aircraft design well beyond the war itself and into the next decade.

A handsome craft, its thick, almost cantilever wings were made of wood and fabric, with welded steel-tube construction for the fuselage. Powered by a 160-horsepower Mercedes engine, the Fokker D VII had a top speed of 120 miles per hour and a ceiling of 23,000 feet. Other planes of the time might top those performance statistics, but the D VII was a forgiving airplane in flight. It was said that the D VII made good pilots out of bad ones and aces out of those who were good to start with.

Why was it important for an airplane to be "forgiving"? To understand that, one has to realize that while rapid advances were made in aviation and airplane design in a very short period during World War I, airplanes were still a very long way from being safe or easy to fly. Pilot training was often very limited, and the planes of those times required constant attention from the pilot just to stay airborne. Aside from the dangers of combat, there were structural problems and related dangers with many planes themselves. Few planes had any devices for maintaining speed or level flight.

The German Gotha bombers, for example, were so tail-heavy that the pilots often would become physically fatigued trying to keep the plane steady during a landing and would crash. The engine in the Sopwith Camel had a tendency to cut out and thus killed many student pilots during takeoff. The lower wing of the Albatros fighters was known to twist away in a dive; and there was constant danger of gasoline fires from the engines of all the planes. Faced with the certainty of a crash with no parachutes, pilots would sometimes shoot themselves rather than burn to death in a gasoline fire from an exploding engine.

So it is not hard to see that while the necessities of World War I provided a push to aviation engineering and development, the very rapid development of new aircraft in those years had its negative side. Pilot safety took a back seat to efficiency in battle and many, many lives were lost. But without the war, aviation never would have come so far in so short a span of time. The war forced progress because of necessity—and the next decade would see that progress evaluated, digested, and improved upon. In the years that followed, the engineers who emerged from World War I would cluster in groups all over the world, plotting the future of flying with new designs, new test flights, and unflagging vision.

Muddy French training fields were the first stop for most young American pilots. However, in any unit, the vast majority of personnel were not pilots but support staff—mechanics and other ground crew who kept the relatively few pilots in the air. Overleaf: a SPAD XIII at the National Air and Space Museum. The tombstone markings, just visible under the wing, indicate the number of missions flown. The shooting star insignia identifies the 22nd Aero Pursuit Squadron.

THE GOLDEN AGE

The years between World War I and World War II have been called the Golden Age of Aviation. During these years, the airplane would grow far beyond the initial developments of World War I into an age in which aviation would never again be thought of as solely a sport for aristocrats or a new tool for the military. In the decades between the two wars, people would for the first time realize the airplane's potential for more ordinary uses to benefit the world.

Many of the engineers and pilots who survived World War I came out of it determined to turn aviation into a real industry. They had seen what government money and production could do to advance the development of airplanes and were convinced that now that the war was over, the same could be done in private industry. Back home in their native countries, especially in the United States, these early aviators and engineers set about establishing small, progressive companies that would prove to be the foundation of the airline industry as we know it today.

The nineteen twenties and thirties were decades when individual ambition was reinforced by national pride. Formerly embattled nations were at last able to celebrate their heroes, and they did—in the newspapers, on the radio, with parades.

The veterans brought back from Europe a glamorous image, based on their bravery in

Airfields of the early twenties hosted civilian pilots of the U.S. Post Office Department and, later, employees of private contractors. Wilma Wethington's painting, "Threatening Weather But the Mail Must Go Through," captures the determined spirit of the early Air Mail Service.

combat. The aura of mystery and daring that followed them worked to their advantage in establishing the aviation industry all over the world. The idea of flight was in keeping with the adventurous and romantic spirit of the times; aviators and their airplanes captured the popular imagination almost immediately—and the veterans did what they could to capitalize on that.

New inventions and improvements in aircraft flourished and were applauded by the public. It was an attitude far removed from the scorn and derision the Wright brothers had experienced in their first experiments. People now not only believed in the future of the airplane, they took it to their hearts.

Before long, the aviation industry attained wonderful momentum, spurred by swiftly advancing developments in the science of aerodynamics, developments which, in turn, would bring profound changes in design, structure, engines, equipment, and piloting technique. Aviation was a field to which a war-weary world could turn with enthusiasm. There were records to be broken, first flights to be made, races to be won. In those days, an air race was the equivalent of the world series or a championship boxing match. The contests were closely followed, the contestants cele-

brated for their abilities. The champion of such a race was sure to become famous overnight. It was a time when anyone could catapult himself (or herself) into fame and fortune with a single winning flight or design. An airline manufacturer who housed his company in a garage might suddenly make a million dollars selling the company's stock after one of his planes won a race.

Perhaps the most famous of these overnight celebrities was a man named Charles Lindbergh. Born in 1902, Lindbergh was only slightly older than aviation itself, and in the minds and hearts of people everywhere, he seemed to sum up all the glamour and daring of his times. Beyond his reputation as a dashing and brave aviator, he was a man who never faltered in his search for technical excellence. His easygoing style and winning ways masked a true perfectionist, a man who really knew his airplanes. Lindbergh began his career in aviation as a parachutist, later became an army pilot, and then flew as an airmail pilot, experience that would lay the foundation for his subsequent achievements.

Though being an airmail pilot might not seem impressive by today's standards, in the nineteen twenties it was considered as daring and romantic a profession as one could imag-

Young people of the twenties equated flight with freedom and romance. Opposite, this young woman appeared on a poster announcing "The First International Aero Congress" in Omaha, Nebraska, in 1921. In the East, especially at such Ivy League schools as Harvard, college boys, top, formed groups to share the high costs of aviation. And the rugged airmail men thrilled the hearts of American women, as suggested by the poster above.

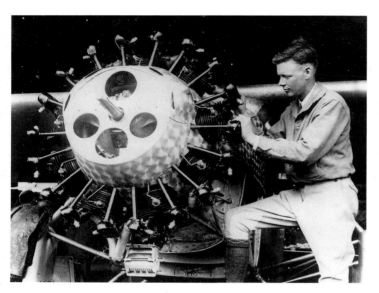

Charles Lindbergh, top, was adamant in his quest for technical excellence, a trait that led him to the Ryan Company of San Diego for the design and construction of his Spirit of St. Louis. *Without the new Wright J-5 Whirlwind engine, above, Lindbergh's flight in 1927 might well have met with disaster.*

ine. But airmail service was more than just glamorous. In fact, its establishment in the United States in many ways marked the beginnings of the aviation industry in America. The first coast-to-coast airmail service was established as early as 1918, but the Contract Air Mail Act, or Kelley Act, of 1925, provided that airmail service be transferred to private operators on a competitive bidding basis. Private companies were then paid by the government to fly the mail. It was an example of the kind of exchange that would go on between government and government contracts and the fledgling aviation industry. By turning airmail service over to private contractors, the government ensured the futures of the companies involved. The pilots of the day, Lindbergh included, were touted as dashing and heroic figures, but they were also among the most experienced fliers of their time. Flying as much as he did for the airmail service, Lindbergh knew his planes from the inside out—and he was always on the lookout for new and better equipment.

At this time, most aircraft still made use of the in-line, liquid-cooled engines that had predominated during World War I. Lindbergh, like any pilot of his day, was well aware of the dangers and unreliability of these engines. So when he first learned of the development by the Wright Aeronautical Corporation of an air-cooled radial aircraft engine, known as the Wright J-5 Whirlwind, which promised greater reliability and eliminated cooling-system maintenance problems, he was farsighted enough to know that this development

The Spirit of St. Louis *was, basically, a flying gasoline tank with a superb engine. After the nonstop flight to Paris and visits to other countries, the aircraft was brought home to a place of honor in the Smithsonian collections. Today it is displayed at the National Air and Space Museum.*

in particular constituted the wave of the future. For the first time, aircraft had a really dependable source of power.

Lindbergh subsequently went to the Ryan Company of San Diego to help design and build an airplane to include the revolutionary new engine. The remarkable plane that resulted, the *Spirit of St. Louis,* would carry him to triumph. When a man named Raymond Orteig offered $25,000 to the first pilot to fly nonstop between New York and Paris, in either direction, Lindbergh and the *Spirit of St. Louis* were ready. Though he was the seventy-ninth person to cross the Atlantic by air, his was the first solo, nonstop leap between the North American and European mainlands. On completion of the flight in May 1927, Charles Augustus Lindbergh was an international hero. People everywhere celebrated him and his amazing trip. There was even a popular song written about him, "Charlie Is My Darling." His triumphant return to New York was celebrated with an enormous ticker-tape parade, an event that would set the style for countless parades to come, and the world, it seemed, was at his feet. Together with his wife, Anne Morrow Lindbergh, whom he taught to be an avid aviator, Lindbergh went on to survey the first air routes to Europe and even to exotic and mysterious parts of the Far East, destinations that had never before seemed imaginable. Lindbergh would continue to figure prominently in American aviation, using his influence to set in motion economic and legislative initiatives that would affect aviation for years to come.

Having seen the future of the airplane during the war, many governments continued military research and expenditure on aircraft development after the war was over. To support the establishment of aviation in private industry, some governments began to offer financial benefits to companies involved in aviation research and improvement. Yet, since this was peacetime, government spending was kept at relatively low levels, and not a great many *new* aircraft were produced for military purposes, at least until the mid-thirties. What happened instead was a healthy exchange between the military and private industry. Each of the countries leading in aviation at the time followed almost the same pattern, establishing centers to undertake the aviation research and development necessary for military purposes. These centers would subsequently do business with private manufacturers.

In the United States, there were three of these: the center for Army Air Service development, at McCook Field in Dayton, Ohio; the Naval Aircraft Factory in Philadelphia; and the National Advisory Committee for Aeronautics, (NACA, the ancestor of NASA) in Langley, Virginia. The first two of these centers engaged in limited production, but for the most part they made their research results available to private industry through publication and, even more often, by putting their designs up for manufacture bids by private contractors. In this way (as had happened with the airmail service contracts), any number of small companies were kept alive by government money and were encouraged to create

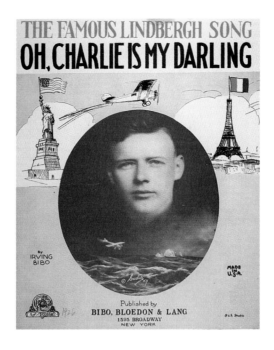

THE FAMOUS LINDBERGH SONG
OH, CHARLIE IS MY DARLING

By IRVING BIBO

Published by
BIBO, BLOEDON & LANG
1595 BROADWAY
NEW YORK

Overnight, the unknown Lindbergh became the world's darling—acclaimed in every way, including songs written about him, left.

their own designs as well. It was a case of one hand washing the other; governments had to limit their military spending, and by using small companies for production were able to keep spending down. Small private companies in turn were kept in business with government contracts and so were able to continue to develop and advance their own designs. It was in this atmosphere that a number of important manufacturing companies began to emerge; McDonnell-Douglas, Lockheed, and Boeing are still in existence today.

But despite this hand-in-hand relationship, the developments in aircraft designed for the military fell far behind the developments coming out of private industry. New developments in military aircraft at the time centered mostly on added equipment: oxygen tanks for pilots, radio gear, bomb racks, and so on. Airframe weight soared and performance plunged. Private designers, in the meantime, were making great strides in performance, design, and construction principles.

This imbalance became clear during the 1929 National Air Races. Military aircraft had dominated this particular event for a number of years and the army Curtiss Hawk P-3a was again favored as the victor. But instead the

winning craft was the truly remarkable civilian Model R Mystery Ship, built by a man named Walter Beech. In a single flight, the Model R Mystery Ship revolutionized the industry, and civilian designs would dominate the races both at home and abroad for nearly a decade.

The Model R was the first plane with an aircooled radial engine to exceed 200 miles per hour. The sleek engine cowling was designed by Fred Weick, working for the NACA. Basically, this cowling, an aerodynamic feature, enclosing, or at least partially enclosing, the engine itself, served to cut the friction, or "drag," of air rushing around the flat shape of a radial engine.

Two other significant developments to occur in these years were the design of improved liquid-cooled engines and the development of a controllable-pitch propeller. As was often the case, one led to the other. The liquid-cooled engines utilized ethylene glycol (Prestone) coolant instead of water, and featured in-line cylinders that made for leaner snouts on the aircraft, in contrast to the bulbous noses required to house the bulkier radial engines. The leaner design reduced drag and the Prestone liquid cooling allowed for higher operating

The Travel Air Model R Mystery Ship, left, was a harbinger of aircraft to come. At the National Air Races in 1929 it vanquished even the military entries, winning the free-for-all speed competition. One innovation, visible here, is the NACA cowling, surrounding its radial engine, which cut wind resistance.

temperatures. Yet it was clear to everyone that the key to unlocking performance was to create an adjustable-pitch propeller. The fixed-pitch propeller that had been in use since the Wright brothers was limiting because it was designed for maximum speed. It was not efficient for take-off and cruising. Ground-adjustable propellers helped, but the real breakthrough came with the development of in-flight propeller control. In the United States, a man named Frank Caldwell led the way, but once again there were parallel developments all over the world.

By 1929, then, the aviation industry had learned almost everything it needed to know to pave the way for the great airplanes of the thirties. And in the ten years preceding World War II, aviation would really take its rightful place in the world with the development of new and sophisticated military equipment as well as the firm establishment of passenger airlines.

In America, many feared that the Great Depression, which began with the stock-market crash in October of 1929, would halt aviation development in this country; but although many companies did go under in those troubled times, many not only remained in busi-

ness but prospered. Part of the reason for this continued prosperity was the growing science of aeronautical engineering. Under this new scientific discipline, the old (and expensive) trial-and-error methods of the Wright brothers and their contemporaries gradually disappeared and were replaced by systematic and scientific study that occurred *prior* to the actual construction of an aircraft. This meant that manufacturers not only saved time, but also saved money in an era when there was not a lot of money to go around.

A basic part of aeronautical engineering is the study of the motion of air and other gases and the effects of this motion on objects moving through them at various heights and speeds. The ability to calculate these effects mathematically allowed engineers to develop airplanes that took advantage of them. Most of these new engineers were aviators themselves. By 1930 a number of them had added academic honors to their aviator's wings.

Perhaps the best known of these was James Doolittle, whose doctor of science in aeronautics from Massachusetts Institute of Technology prepared him for a lifetime of scientific achievement. Yet Doolittle's piloting feats were so remarkable that they have almost overshadowed his scientific accomplishments. He won races, set records, and led the 1942 aircraft carrier–launched raid against Tokyo. In the scientific arena, he helped pioneer instrument flight and worked to develop 100-octane aviation fuel, among other accomplishments.

It was an exciting time in an exciting field. In the early days of aeronautics, it was possible to combine intuition with science to achieve major breakthroughs. A designer could make use of his scientific calculations, yet still have the freedom to play his hunches. And a great many wonderful planes emerged as a result. One of the best examples was built by multimillionaire industrialist and moviemaker Howard Hughes. His H-1 racer is, many believe, the most beautiful piston-engine aircraft ever made. And with Hughes's insistence on perfection, the H-1 proved itself to be more than merely beautiful. It set the speed record for a measured course in 1935 and would go on to set the transcontinental speed record in 1937, averaging 327 miles per hour between Los Angeles and Newark, New Jersey.

Though their work may not have achieved the fame and recognition that Hughes's and Lindbergh's did, private designers made a number of important contributions too. William Piper, collaborating with C. G. Taylor, first began to market one of the most successful light planes of the period, the famous Piper Cubs, many of which are still being flown today.

People became more and more interested in air travel, which spawned two new additions to the field of transport: the great dirigible transport ships and flying boats, both of which promised their customers all the luxury of an ocean liner in the air. The dirigibles unfortunately failed to overcome the problems that had plagued the design since its invention, namely that hydrogen gas is highly inflammable. While helium was available and much safer than hydrogen, its sale to Germany was prohibited. As a result, a number of those airships that relied on hydrogen gas for lift incurred disaster, including the explosion and crash of the German *Hindenberg* on May 6, 1937.

The flying boats were much safer. Introduced by Glenn Curtiss as early as 1911, they were, for many years, preeminent for overwater flight. It was easier to land a flying boat on the water than to build an airport, not to mention less expensive. Many types of flying boats were produced in limited quantity, but none were so grand as America's Pan American China Clippers and the unsurpassed Boeing 314 Clipper. Flying boats continued to be used all through World War II, but their use declined after that. The war itself had brought about the construction of airports all over the world, and greater advances in four-engine land aircraft made them obsolete.

The prosperity of the aviation industry in America during the thirties was also supported by America's emergence as a leader in the passenger-airline industry. European passenger transport had been in existence since

the end of World War I. Military planes had been used to transport dignitaries back and forth from the peace conferences, and there followed the beginnings of an airline industry as wealthy and fashionable aristocrats discovered flying as a means of travel. But America's large and efficient railway system served to offset the need for air travel in this country—as did her geographical size. Distances between neighboring countries in Europe are relatively short; they could be flown with less efficient aircraft and shorter flying times. But the land area in America is huge by comparison; to establish regular air routes in this

tion, cantilevered wings, retractable landing gear, and neatly cowled engines. In fact, though, the new aircraft had what might be called a major flaw—it was too small! On the advice of its pilot experts, Boeing had designed the plane so it could carry only ten passengers, perhaps believing that no more were necessary since so few people traveled by air. Still, the plane was so advanced that United Air Lines bought the first sixty of the 247s anyway.

Another company, Transcontinental & World Airlines (TWA), was at that time having safety problems with some of its own craft and requested that another manufacturer, Douglas Aircraft, respond to the 247 with a design of their own. The first of these was the DC-1 (of which only one was built), then came the fourteen-seat DC-2, and finally, the twenty-one-seat DC-3, which came on the scene in 1936, only three years after the 247.

The DC-3 was everything the Boeing 247 was and more. It was the basis for the growth of commercial airlines all over the world and it shortly proved itself to be the first plane able to make a profit for commercial airlines without their having to take on mail routes as they had in the past. In short, it was the plane that could support an entire industry. Five years after its appearance, the DC-3 provided 80 percent of domestic scheduled service, a near-monopoly due in part to its strong safety record. America produced between twelve thousand and thirteen thousand civilian and military DC-3s. Its design was copied all over the world. In Russia, Japan, France, and Italy,

country simply required better planes for passenger transport than were available in the twenties. As a result, the very factors that had held civil aviation back in the beginning steadily forced American designers to come up with more advanced aircraft, and they did just that, beginning with Boeing's 247, first put into service in 1933.

Based on innovations for a Boeing bomber design called the B-9, the Boeing 247 first appeared in February of 1933 and instantly set the new industry standard. Suddenly every other passenger transport in the world was obsolete. The 247 featured all-metal construc-

its lines were copied so closely that it was difficult to tell the difference. Yet in the case of the DC-3, the copies never improved on or even equaled the original. No one was able to match the performance or the durability of the American product.

Yet it was understandable that while America was dominating the passenger-airline industry, Europe would fall behind in the area of commercial airline development. For during the last half of the nineteen thirties, Europeans were once again turning an eye to more serious uses for their airplanes and concentrating on the development of military aircraft. With the emergence of Hitler's Germany, war again loomed on Europe's horizon, and with every new plane to come out of Germany it was clear that the formation of a German air force, the famed and hated Luftwaffe, was only moments away.

WORLD WAR II: REAPING THE WHIRLWIND

Though Hitler's threat to the rest of the world was a real one, in its initial stages another world war was difficult to imagine. German military spending and rearmament had been severely limited by the Treaty of Versailles, which marked the end of World War I. It took some time before anyone realized the treaty was not being honored. After 1934, Hitler's Germany began rebuilding its military capability with the development and training of ground forces, the Wermacht, as well as the reestablishment of an air force, the Reichsluftwaffe or Luftwaffe. Much of this was done in secret, of course, because such development violated the treaty. Fighter pilots received their initial training in ordinary gliders, and the Germans insisted they were only building transport planes when they introduced the Heinkel He 111, the Dornier Do 17, and the advanced Focke Wulf Fw 200 Condor. The Condor accommodated twenty-six passengers and broke records with its round-trip flight to New York in 1938. The Condor would also serve the Luftwaffe as a bombing and reconnaissance plane. By the time Germany produced the design for the Junkers Ju 87 Stuka, a dive bomber, there could no longer be any doubt as to the re-emergence of German air power.

In the years just prior to the outbreak of World War II, what many people feared most was an air war. Perhaps they did not see Hitler's true intentions simply because they did

Memories of war in the air, here is a collection of war memorabilia from both Smithsonian and private collections.

not want to. The world had seen how airplanes, fighters, and bombers changed the face of World War I, and fully believed that with the technological advances and improvements that had occurred since then, a worldwide conflict in the air would mean something very close to the end of the world. In a way, people then felt the same way about a large-scale air war as people feel today about the possibility of nuclear warfare.

In fact, Germany began her offensive with a propaganda program that was far more efficient than the air force actually was. In 1936, Hitler's feared Luftwaffe boasted only around two hundred obsolete aircraft, including the Dornier Do 23 and the bomber version of the Junkers Ju 52. Each of these airplanes could haul 2,000 pounds of bombs or travel a distance of 800 miles, but they couldn't do both on the same mission. In fact, it wasn't until near the end of World War II that bombers could be judged to hit specific targets. Yet both the British and French governments trembled in their boots, convinced by Hitler's propaganda that the Germans, and the Italians (who, with Japan, were soon to be allied with Germany), could deliver devastating blows from the air. The Luftwaffe did what it could to reinforce a sense of terror. Inadequate and obsolete as it was, the Luftwaffe intimidated the world as never before. It was a favorite ploy of both the Italians and the Germans to shuttle the same aircraft, sometimes hastily repainted, from field to field to better impress visiting military leaders with their numbers. After being taken on a dazzling tour of one

such airfield, a French chief-of-staff returned to France and reported that, should war with Germany come, the entire French Air Force would be wiped out within a week—a prediction that would prove uncomfortably close to correct later on.

So convinced of this were the soon-to-be Allied powers (England, France, the United States, and later, the Soviet Union), that these governments began intensive research and development programs for military aircraft, bombers in particular. As the threat grew, the Allies began to rearm at a pace that to many may have seemed impossible. But this rearmament would eventually make a crucial difference in winning the war. At drafting tables all over the world, engineers sought different solutions to different problems. With war imminent, it was no longer enough to create a design with a competitive performance. The aircraft also had to be mass-produced, and easy to repair and maintain, especially under field conditions—lessons first learned in World War I.

Germany, among the leaders in design innovation in the thirties, produced the Messerschmitt Bf 109 fighter, equipped with a 700-horsepower engine, and descendants of this German design flourished in other countries long after the Luftwaffe folded its wings. More than thirty-three thousand were built and, with its low cantilever wing, retractable landing gear, all-metal construction, and enclosed cockpit, the Messerschmitt Bf 109 in many ways served to set the standard for piston-engine fighting planes of World War II.

France, 1940: Royal Air Force (RAF) pilots of No. 87 Squadron, above, sprint toward their Hawker Hurricane fighters. Although Britain possessed greater numbers of the sturdy but slower Hawker Hurricanes, the nimble Spitfire, overleaf, was her premier World War II fighter and proved to be a match for the versatile German Messerschmitt Bf 109. These carefully restored "Spits" display the clean lines designed by Reginald Mitchell in 1935.

In Britain, two new designs proved to be of special importance: the eight-gun Hawker Hurricane and Spitfire. Both used a 1,000-horsepower Rolls Royce Merlin engine, among the most advanced and powerful of its time. In the United States, a designer named Don Berlin at Curtiss-Wright produced the Hawk 75, which would lead to the P-36, and later to the P-40s, a series of famous fighters with which America would enter the war.

Germany produced one of the most feared and hated planes of the war: the Junkers Ju 87

Stuka, a legendary dive bomber. Soon after, the Luftwaffe began to expand at an incredible rate, but still not quickly enough. By 1939, German aircraft production had reached about seven hundred a month, which the Germans considered adequate for a war they believed would be a short one. Five years later, in 1944, Germany was struggling to produce four thousand planes per month. But by then, that wasn't nearly enough.

Hitler began his offensive on September 1, 1939, when the forces of the Wermacht and

After British units were forced to abandon France in June 1940, "Chain Home" radar stations, like the one below, gave the British vital early warning of German air raids.

though his forces would prove inadequate against the huge resources of the Allies later on, against the unarmed and unsophisticated military forces of traditionally neutral countries such as Norway, the Blitzkrieg seemed unstoppable.

At the time, Britain was closely allied with France, and as Hitler pushed through Belgium and Holland into French territory, British forces in France were cut off from their French allies. Even though Hitler's victories up to that point had been easy ones, his army was nevertheless one of the best-trained the world had ever seen. Both the British and the French found out just how efficient Germany's war machine could be at the famous Battle of Dunkirk. Trampled by Hitler's army, Britain was forced to withdraw her ground forces, and France fell in only six weeks. The French demanded continued air support from Britain, but British Air Chief Marshal Sir Hugh Dowding withdrew his precious fighter squadrons. It was a wise decision, for in the terrible weeks to come, England would need every plane, every pilot, every bullet she had.

The Battle of Britain, in the autumn of 1940, gave the world its first taste of to what extent a full-scale war could go. The destruction was incredible. Until then, Germany had been sending out fighters and dive bombers against countries with little or no air power of their own. But when Hitler made the decision to try to invade England, he came up against an air force that was evenly matched with his own and that was assisted in its defense by developments in radar technology. For a solid

the Luftwaffe, combined into a Blitzkrieg, or "lightning war," slashed into Poland. Poland fell three weeks later. Hitler then invaded Belgium and Holland, intent on pushing next into France. French forces, particularly their air forces, were utterly inadequate, and while they did have bombers at their disposal in 1939, they chose not to use them, perhaps fearing for civilian lives and private property. In the meantime, Hitler, in a series of risky and brilliant strikes, conquered Norway, Denmark, Belgium, and Holland. But it is important to remember that these were easy victories for Hitler. He attacked poorly armed countries with little or no warning, and

three months, the battle was close, fierce, and terrible. British Hurricane and Spitfire fighters, agile and fast, were nearly a perfect counterpart to the German Messerschmitt 109s. Hitler began the day and night bombing of London using Heinkel He 111s and Junkers Ju 88s. The Royal Air Force refused to allow England to be invaded by the Nazi machine. The exploits of the RAF pilots during the three months of the London Blitz prompted Winston Churchill, Prime Minister of England at the time and a hero in his own right, to declare: "Never in the field of human conflict was so much owed by so many to so few."

Perhaps the deciding difference in the battle was in the difference in command. The Luftwaffe had expanded rapidly under Hermann Goering; in the few short years between 1934 and 1939, he had built an air force from a propaganda trick into a machine that terrified the world. It was Goering's practice, as head of the Luftwaffe, to promote his best and bravest pilots to command positions as a reward for their heroism. Yet brave pilots do not always make the best commanders, and as the war expanded, the Luftwaffe began to be plagued by a lack of spare parts and fuel, and by poor pilot training that never would have been tolerated in the RAF. Even as Hitler expanded the conflict by declaring war on Russia and opening up the eastern front, supply and manufacturing chains for the Luftwaffe were beginning to break apart.

But the conflict was far from over; in fact, it was expanding. Italy had entered the war in June of 1940 and, with her proximity to the Middle East and Africa, opened up a whole new set of battlefields. Many countries of that region were either colonies of the English or the French or closely tied to them through alliances and treaties. Italy's air force, though largely obsolete, boasted some beautiful and highly efficient fighters, including the Macchi C. 202, which was elegantly designed and mechanically excellent.

In Asia, Japan had begun an offensive that matched Hitler's for daring and effectiveness. Already at war with China, Japan brought the United States into World War II when she launched a surprise attack by aircraft-carrier-based planes on the great American naval base at Pearl Harbor, Hawaii, on December 7, 1941. Japan's small air force was essentially created as support for both her army and

navy. Yet this relatively small force, flying the Nakajima Ki-43, or the "Oscar" as it was referred to by American pilots, the Mitsubishi A6M1 Zero ("Zeke"), and the G4M ("Betty"), proved to be a ferocious one. Highly trained and disciplined, the Japanese were among the best fighter pilots in the world; pilots who would, as the war progressed, prove their expertise and dedication, even to the point of suicide, in the desperate Kamikaze missions that marked the end of Japanese air power in the Pacific.

The United States did not officially enter the war until the attack on Pearl Harbor in 1941, but American designers and factories had been supplying planes to the Allies for two years. The war provided a substantial boost to aviation manufacture and design in this country. In 1939 America produced only about twenty-two hundred military aircraft a year. By 1944 the number had risen to nearly one hundred thousand per year, some of which were the most complex and efficient machines of their time. The American tradition of industry and teamwork, together with the nation's natural resources, made her well prepared for entry into the conflict, and everyone worked together in a mutual push for production. As men went to war, women did too, taking over the airplane assembly lines and helping to put together the more than three hundred sixty thousand aircraft that were produced during World War II.

As the Allies pulled together in production of aircraft, the Axis powers continued to pull apart. Plagued by shortages of skilled machinists, tools, raw materials, and fuels, Germany was simply not able to continue manufacturing new aircraft, and in some instances could not fly the planes she did produce, simply because there was not enough fuel! Hitler had expanded his war too far and too fast; his resources could not keep up with the demands of his armies. With the addition of the natural resources of a huge country like the United States to the Allied forces, a relatively small country such as Germany simply couldn't compete. Hitler and his advisors, remember, had planned for a short war; in a way, they had set their sights too low to be able to catch up. Japan too should have known better than to overextend the war, but the victory over American forces at Pearl Harbor convinced her leaders that they could. What they encountered instead was an absolutely huge Allied air force. Clearly outnumbered, the Axis

powers struggled on. By 1944, the Allies began to command air superiority in the skies over Europe in planes such as the P-51 Mustang, which many considered to be the best fighter of the war, and bombers such as the B-17, which was capable of carrying a bomb load of six thousand pounds. Also, by 1944, the Grumman F6F Hellcat would figure prominently in the defeat of Japan, as did the B-29, a heavy bomber that represented perhaps one of the most complex engineering feats in history. Unsurpassed in speed and range, enormous fleets of B-29s reduced Japanese cities to rubble.

Artist R. G. Smith, below, pictured U. S. Navy Douglas SBD Dauntless dive bombers flying over the stricken Japanese carrier Akagi *during the pivotal Battle of Midway, June 3–6, 1942. Opposite, forward section of* Flak Bait, *a famed Martin B-26 bomber, now residing at the National Air and Space Museum.* Flak Bait *completed in excess of 200 missions over Europe. More than 1,000 patches on its fuselage hide perforations from shell fragments called* flak, *a word derived from the German word for anti-aircraft cannon.*

No major Axis offensive succeeded after 1943. During 1943, Germany was forced into full retreat from the eastern front. Italy deserted her, and she was thrown out of Africa. Night and day, bombers left their mark on the German countryside, laying factories, supply depots, and transport routes to waste. Japan, too, was failing. Just as she had advanced, island by island, she was forced to retreat in the Pacific. Yet the Japanese fought on relentlessly, giving their lives for what was a hopeless cause.

Though it was too late to save the wounded Third Reich, Germany introduced two technologies that would forecast the future of flight and warfare: the Messerschmitt Me 262, the world's first operational jet fighter, and then the rocket-propelled V-2, the first long-range ballistic missile. Turbojet and rocket technology would later prove to be the foundation

for all modern aircraft and the ballistic missile would take aviation beyond the smoke-blackened skies over Europe and into the spage age.

In the final analysis, Allied pilots and their fine aircraft did not win the war by themselves. But they certainly played a strong role, perhaps a vital role, in the victory over Germany. World War II marked not only the end of the Third Reich but the end of an era in aviation. With the development of precision bombing, radar, and heavy bombers such as the B-29, the world began to realize the capacity for destruction it had only feared in the beginning. Then, in 1945, the Boeing B-29 Superfortress carried to Hiroshima and Nagasaki just two bombs that created destruction more sudden and horrible than anyone had ever imagined possible, and air power instantly took on an entirely new and frightening dimension.

B-17 Flying Fortresses, above, of the 96th Bomb Group, Eighth Air Force, flying through large caliber flak over northern Germany, 1944. At the time of its introduction in 1944, the B-29 bomber, opposite top, was perhaps the most complex engineering achievement in history. Opposite bottom, overwhelmingly defeated, Japanese representatives gathered on the deck of the U.S.S. Missouri to sign the documents of surrender.

Part 3

World War II forever changed the world and the future of aviation. Humankind had faced terrible destruction and had come away with hopes for a better, more peaceful future. In aviation, people experienced much the same burst of enthusiasm that they had felt in the aftermath of World War I. With the brilliant new technologies that had emerged from the war at their disposal, people everywhere could turn their attention toward a new age in which air travel would be commonplace, navigational systems and radar the order of the day, and the push beyond the skies and into space a very real possibility.

The age of jets would release a flood of new technology: more advanced radar, swept-back wings, long-dreamed-of vertical-flight, supersonic speeds, and space shuttles—the list is endless. America would learn, in the context of military conflicts that were to come in Korea and Vietnam, that sometimes the elaborate new systems simply weren't practical under the demanding conditons of combat and that sometimes, at least, it was better to simplify. During the nineteen seventies, inflation and huge jumps in fuel costs would teach aviation to economize: to continue to utilize some of the grand old machines, to spruce them up with fine new systems and send them out again into the skies.

And finally, we learned to dream again about the future of aviation. A future in which the thrill of flight would be given back to the individual in private aircraft so light and economical and easy to fly that anyone who wanted might use them. A future in which supersonic transport could take a place in commercial flight. We dream now of a world where together we discover that our limit is no longer the sky, but the stars.

Most successful of all experimental research aircraft, the North American X-15 was powered by an engine that generated 60,000 pounds of thrust. In 1967 the X-15 rocketed to nearly Mach 7, a speed no other aircraft has ever approached.

THE JET AGE

Of all the Allied and Axis powers, only the United States had no scars from the war on her own soil. America was not faced with the enormous task of rebuilding cities, towns, and factories, and so was perhaps the best equipped, for a number of reasons, to usher the rest of the world into the jet age. Germany had been first in the development and design of turbojet and rocket engines, as well as in some aerodynamic features such as the swept-back wing, but these innovations had come too late to benefit the Germans during the war. After the war was over, German designs and experience became available to the world, and the United States, with its huge factories and enormous resources, was the first nation to take those technologies into production.

After World War II, the world was left with an expanded system of airports and runways, fuel dumps, and navigational and mete-orological facilities. Hundreds of thousands of pilots had been trained during the war, and these, with such worldwide availability of fa-cilities, led to a revolution in aviation—a revo-lution in thinking. If one wanted to go to Africa or India or simply to cross the ocean to Europe, one could now consider going by plane. Flying had become an indisputable real-ity of modern life. World travel became globe-trotting—a matter of hours, not days or weeks. It was no wonder that this postwar era gave rise to the first real flying generation.

The rocket-propelled Bell X-1, piloted by Charles E. "Chuck" Yeager, first broke the sonic barrier in 1947. Yeager named the X-1 Glamorous Glennis *after his wife, and the plane now hangs in the Smithsonian National Air and Space Museum.*

In America, as elsewhere, the demobilization that followed the war meant some hard times for manufacturers, and many of them went out of business. In addition, thousands of surplus aircraft left over from the fighting dotted the landscape at storage fields from Arizona to Australia. Some newly produced aircraft were flown just once—from the factory to storage sites—and abandoned after only five hours in the air. Rumors and legends abounded about the incredible surpluses; there were stories of brand-new P-38s shoved off docks and P-51s buried for landfill. A California stunt pilot named Paul Mantz became the

"ninth-largest air force in the world" by buying an entire fleet of B-17s, B-24s, and other planes, then paying for them by draining the high-octane fuel from their tanks and selling it! The great war planes were put into mothballs or sent to boneyards, or even to the melting pots of salvage yards, where they were smelted for the aluminum in their frames.

Not having to rebuild was one factor in America's dominance of postwar aviation; another reason America led the way was that she had to. Much of the American economic recovery from the Great Depression was a result of the tremendous industrial growth that oc-

Many military aircraft, like the C-47s (the military version of the DC-3) were "mothballed" after the war. Many, however, reemerged in airline livery service, and some still fly today.

curred during World War II, including airplane manufacture. Simply shutting down the aviation industry would surely be harmful to the American economy. To rely on surplus war planes for military and commercial needs during peacetime would not only slow the progress of aviation, it would mean the loss of countless jobs and companies throughout the country. In order to avoid that, it became necessary for American military and industrial concerns to bind together once again, just as they had during the years following World War I. Manufacturing and development of aircraft continued, even if it was only at a frac-

tion of its wartime rate. This new military-industrial complex, as President Eisenhower dubbed it in the late nineteen fifties, demanded that the technological momentum created by the war be kept up, and the "cold war" was a threat that encouraged Congress to continue military funding.

In this climate, military planners and industrialists began their own push for research and development of new aircraft. The orders were small compared to what they had been during the war, but the technological advances that they would engender would prove incredible.

The jet engine was the focal point for new

aviation technology. Developed at about the same time in Britain and Germany, it comprised a milestone in aviation history. Unlike the old piston engine, the jet engine's source of power is the turbine, a rotating device that draws air into the engine, compresses it, mixes it with fuel, and ignites the mixture. The compressed fuel-air mixture is expelled in exhaust, providing thrust, and therefore propulsion.

At first, jet engines were comparatively low powered. But they rapidly grew more powerful. Just as propeller-driven airplanes had been developed with first one engine, then two, three, and four, designers began to create huge and powerful jet-propelled planes that boasted as many as six or even eight jet engines, striving for the greatest possible performance from the largest possible airframe.

This new source of power also made it possible to revolutionize aerodynamic design. Just as the development of the NACA cowling had reduced the drag from the large, flat noses of radial engines, the jet engines required different aerodynamics for efficiency. The first American jet bomber, the XB-43 (the X stood for experimental), was a completely conventional bomber design, except that it had jet engines. Nevertheless, refinements and experiments continued, and before long a fighter, the American XP-86 Sabre, featured wings and tail swept back at 35-degree angles. Swept wings would prove a great leap forward in jet design because the angle significantly reduced drag and improved performance around the speed of sound.

The late forties were also years when more and more people were learning the convenience and advantages of air travel, and before long the first modern commercial airliners began to appear. In June of 1947, Pan American Airlines began round-the-world service in the "Connie," Lockheed's elegant L-749 Constellation. This same plane would serve TWA and American Overseas Airlines as intercontinental air routes proliferated during peacetime. Even though competition from other countries gradually increased as the years passed, the U.S. reigned supreme in commercial transport in the years following World War II. Planes like the Connie or Boeing's luxurious double-decker passenger plane, the 377 Stratocruiser, were well designed for their roles. Another star of the postwar passenger planes was the Douglas C-54, which with many changes would go through a number of civilian designations and model numbers, including the DC-4, DC-6, DC-6A, DC-6B, DC-7, DC-7A, DC-7B and DC-7C! In many ways, these new passenger planes were truly modern, but they did not have jet engines. They still used piston engines driving propellers.

Military aviation also prospered. On September 17, 1947, President Harry Truman signed legislation making the U.S. Air Force a separate branch of the armed services. Prior to that, the air force had been a branch of the army. Under the auspices of NACA (soon to become NASA), the Research Airplane Program proved the cutting edge of aeronautical experimentation. In 1947, the Bell X-1 rocket research airplane succeeded in doing what

Lockheed's elegant Constellation L.749 served Pan American, TWA, and American Overseas Airlines as intercontinental airlines proliferated during peacetime. Pan American opened the first round-the-world service with the "Connie" on June 17, 1947.

The blunt-nosed Boeing 377 Stratocruiser, top, competed with Lockheed's Constellation and shared design features with B-29 and B-50 bombers. Bottom, passengers enjoyed the comfort of this double-decker, which provided berths for transatlantic flights and a lower-deck cocktail bar.

many had thought impossible. Flown by Captain Charles—"Chuck"—Yeager, the Bell X-1 broke the sound barrier. For the first time, an aircraft had traveled faster than the speed of sound. Speed itself could be measured in new terms, not in miles per hour, but in Mach numbers, which measure the speed of a moving body in relation to the speed of sound. Though it does vary according to altitude, Mach 1 is approximately 750 miles per hour at sea level.

Also produced for the military during 1947 was the Boeing B-47 Stratojet bomber, perhaps the most important military jet aircraft of all time because of its influence on world events and future aircraft design. It combined 35-degree swept wings with six jet engines housed in four underwing pods. Although the B-47 did have some problems, such as a long take-off run on a hot day, its good qualities far outweighed the bad. Among its other features, the B-47 had very sophisticated bombing systems and traveled at speeds that made interception by fighter planes more difficult. Also, the B-47 was perhaps one of the first examples of a "defensive weapon" to be produced during peacetime. Capable, impressive, and clearly superior, it might be said that the B-47 was an early example of the nuclear deterrent.

Yet, other countries were not far behind in developing military aircraft. The Soviet Union surprised everyone when it introduced the MiG-15 jet fighter, considered the equal of America's new F-86 Sabre. England and France responded with fine fighters of their own design.

A B-47 Stratojet medium-range bomber blasts off from Edwards Air Force Base with a boost from JATO (Jet—actually rocket—Assisted Take Off).

The MiG-15 and the F-86 Sabre met in combat in the skies over Korea from 1950 through 1953. Communist China came to the aid of the North Koreans and the Soviet Union supplied North Korea with arms and military aid, including the MiG-15 and pilots. Though the performance statistics for the two planes were similar, combat proved otherwise. Roughly thirteen MiG-15s were lost for each Sabre shot down during the Korean conflict. Most of this can be explained by differences in pilot training and skill, but many point out that the Sabre possessed a superior gun platform.

Along with jet technology, there were other revolutions taking place in the development of postwar aircraft. Ever since the days of Leonardo da Vinci's airscrew, aviation enthusiasts had been fascinated with the notion of an aircraft that could take off and land vertically—but the problems of design had seemed insurmountable. Again, Germany had provided the world with the technology necessary for helicopter development as early as 1936, with the Focke-Achgelis Fa 61, considered by many to be the first fully controllable helicopter.

In the United States, a Russian named Igor Sikorsky, an airplane designer, had developed the VS-300, a prototype that would give rise to many succeeding generations of helicopters. Interestingly enough, though, production of helicopters didn't become really practical until after the war, when jet engines made helicopters safer and more efficient.

All-jet or pure-jet power did not come to commercial airliners until 1952, when a British company, de Havilland, introduced the Comet 1A. A beautiful jet liner, the Comet carried thirty-six passengers and traveled at a cruising speed of 500 miles-per-hour. The British inaugurated service between London and Johan-

The American F-86 Sabre, left, was a formidable opponent for the Russian-built MiG-15s, below, as they encountered one another in "MiG Alley" over Korea. Part of the Sabre's superiority can be attributed to greater U. S. pilot experience. By the war's end, ten MiGs had been lost to every Sabre. Opposite, the British de Havilland's Comet, the first commercial jet transport. The Comet's early acclaim was cut short when several crashes caused the public to shun the aircraft.

nesburg, South Africa, and right from the first, the Comet 1A looked like a world-beater. Just as the British had hoped, orders from commercial airline companies poured in. For a time, it looked as though American manufacturers would be left behind in the race for airliner superiority.

Yet it was not to be. Disaster struck when, in January 1954, and again in April of that year, two of the Comets broke up in flight. De Havilland's engineers isolated metal fatigue as the problem—the Comet's fuselage simply could not withstand repeated pressurization. De Havilland redesigned the aircraft to correct the problem, but by then it was too late. The public believed the Comets unsafe and most commercial airlines stopped ordering them.

The Boeing company stepped into the gap left by the Comet when it introduced the world's first successful jet transport: the Boeing 367-80, the prototype for the Boeing 707 in 1954. This incredible jet liner was produced at a cost of more than $16 million, yet despite the financial risks, Boeing's gamble paid off. It was as much of an improvement on the Comet in engineering and design as the Comet itself had been an improvement over piston-engine aircraft. The 707 was designed to come as

Boeing's $16,000,000 gamble, the 367-80, was the prototype for the remarkable Boeing 707. By 1967, 568 Boeing 707s were in use by such airlines as Pan Am, Quantas, and American.

close as possible to the speed of sound and yet to maintain fuel economy. Even today, few subsonic transports are faster. Most still travel at speeds first attained by the 707.

The transition from piston-engine-powered planes to pure jet propulsion was not without problems, though, even for the 707. Much as they admired the 707, many airline companies were reluctant to order any. The huge jets, sleek and impressive as they were, were also extremely expensive. Luckily, the air force came through with a contract for a number of KC-135s (the military tanker version of the 707), and Boeing was able to continue production as, gradually, orders for the new jet liners began to come in. Before long, the quality of the aircraft outweighed its expense, and Boeing had more orders for 707s than it could fill.

As advanced as American aviation was in some areas, it continued to lag behind in others, especially in the development of light-planes and private aircraft. Many flight enthusiasts insisted that soon there would be an airplane in every American garage, yet it was a dream that did not come true. The war

had created hundreds of thousands of military pilots, and manufacturers believed that those pilots would want to own their own planes as they reentered civilian life. The lightplane industry geared up for a boom that in 1947 produced more than seventeen thousand light-planes, including Cessnas, Pipers, and the wonderful Beech Bonanza with its distinctive V-tail styling. But after an initial burst of

acceptance and enthusiasm, sales fell dramatically. Even though they never gained widespread sales, many of the lightplanes designed during the early postwar years are still on the market, unsurpassed in performance or quality.

By 1955, the period of postwar growth had settled in and flight for many people had become almost routine. Yet conditions were right for a new spurt in aviation's growth, and when it came it would prove to be more demanding, rigorous, and challenging to everyone involved than any foregoing period in aviation. From financiers to engineers to pilots, all rose to greater challenges in the coming years, producing aircraft and finally even spacecraft that were bigger, better, and faster than the world had yet seen.

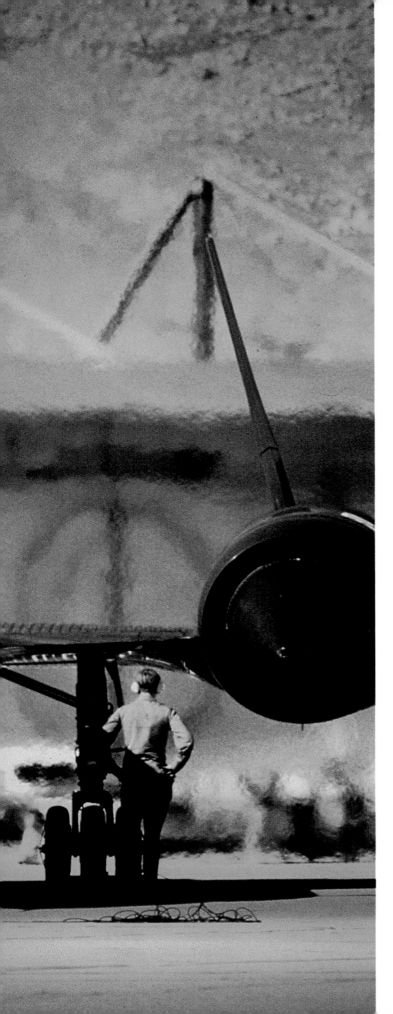

BIGGER, BETTER, FASTER

Aircraft of the nineteen fifties and sixties all went farther, higher, and faster than any that had gone before. But what made this period of progress truly special was that it gave rise to a wider spectrum of improvements than ever before, in aerodynamic innovation and in support technology as well.

Up to this point, advances in aviation had tended to occur in cycles. A giant leap forward, such as the development of a reliable radial engine, was followed by a period during which support for the new equipment emerged, in this case engine cowling to reduce drag. Another example is the invention of the jet engine, which was succeeded by aerodynamic improvements, including swept wings that allowed the jet to be used more effectively. In short, the history of aviation had demonstrated a repeated pattern of giant steps followed by periods when support technology hurried to catch up with smaller but very important improvements. And those, in turn, led to other great leaps in technology.

As flight moved into the jet age, though, the pattern of "giant steps" followed by "catching up" was no longer observed. As pure-jet and turboprop technology became the basis on which most commercial and military aircraft were built, the pattern began to change. Perhaps the most important reason for this is that since the dawn of the twentieth century all sorts of technology had grown just as rapidly

The SR-71, successor to the U-2 reconnaissance plane, can maintain speeds of Mach 3 and fly at an altitude of more than 80,000 feet. It was designed by Lockheed's Clarence "Kelly" Johnson and features a basic structure of titanium and high-temperature plastics.

Cutting in his afterburner, an F-4 Phantom II pilot suddenly doubles his acceleration. The added thrust comes from the injection of fuel into hot exhaust gasses.

as aviation had. By the nineteen fifties and sixties, aviation could be combined with other technologies in ways that had never before been possible. Innovations in performance and design began to be matched by an equal or greater number of innovations in support technology. Structural design progress slowed down, while engineering of the components that went into an airframe increased.

So by the nineteen sixties, advancements in such elements as airframe components and engine performance had been equalled by improvements in navigation, radar, safety, and fire control, and, for military aircraft, bombing, and other weapons control. For the first time, the computer came to the aid of the designers, and later the pilots, of these hot new ships. The fifties and sixties saw the emergence of highly sophisticated military aircraft such as the Navy's F-4 Phantom II fighter, designed especially for air-to-air missile combat. In commercial planes, it was an era that would continue the trend toward large passenger jets such as the Boeing 727 and, later on, wide-body models including the 747, which would carry as many as five hundred passengers, along with other wide-bodies like the Douglas DC-10 and Lockheed's L1011.

Yet as sophisticated and specialized as this new generation of aircraft became, they also required immense supply and maintenance systems. In a way, the commercial aviation industry found itself in much the same kind of situation that had been encountered when military use of the airplanes grew during World War I: no one truly realized the extent of sup-

*Painters at Lockheed paint an L-1011 TriStar, a
wide-bodied jet suitable for cross-country service.*

port network required to supply and maintain aircraft for the battlefield. On a much larger scale, that is what happened as new and infinitely more complex aircraft became available to the entire world, both in commercial travel and especially in the military. In a relatively short period, the maintenance time required per hour of flight increased tenfold as sophisticated radars, gun and missile guidance equipment, and communication and navigation systems became standard in new aircraft. Each of these new developments required extensive research and test equipment, technical manuals, calibration equipment, sources for spare parts, and specially trained mechanics. These new systems require more time in maintenance than the basic airframe.

Another thing the creation and maintenance of modern airplanes and support technology requires is money—lots and lots of it—a factor that has slowed the production of new aircraft dramatically. During World War II, Boeing produced B-17 bombers at a cost of just under two hundred thousand dollars each. Today, the U.S. B-1B bombers cost hundreds of millions dollars each! Yet while new production has steadily declined, the situation does have its advantages. In striving to make use of what we already have, people have come to see aircraft as having much longer lives than they used to. The world has learned to appreciate the flexibility of a good flying machine.

A modern airplane can be changed without changing the basic airframe. Old, obsolete interior equipment can be taken out and new systems built in, without having to construct an entirely new aircraft. In this way, good airplanes can stay in service longer, and special military equipment, sophisticated new computer technology, and, in the case of commercial airliners, even more seats and passengers can be accommodated. Not only are we forced to use what we have to best advantage, but also the system may ensure that only the best ideas make it into production. In many instances, the innovations of the fifties and sixties taught that when it comes to modern aircraft, "more" is not always better: that not all the newest and most advanced technology at our disposal is necessary to make a good aircraft. The military jet fighters are a good example. During the sixties, fighter planes capable of Mach 2 or more appeared all over the world. Yet, in the skies over Vietnam, it was proven that modern aerial combat usually takes place at .9 Mach or less.

Vietnam offered a number of other important insights about jets as the military utilized, under combat conditions, many of our most advanced jet fighters and bombers: F-4 Phantom IIs, B-52s, and others. The North Vietnamese had only a small number of fighters and no bombers, but a very sophisticated anti-aircraft network. The conflict taught the United States a great deal about air power in the age of jets, missiles, and powerful radar systems. Designers learned, for example, that air-to-air missiles were not enough to rid the sky of enemy jets, and that fighters (as the pilots already knew) still needed to be equipped with guns. Furthermore, it became obvious

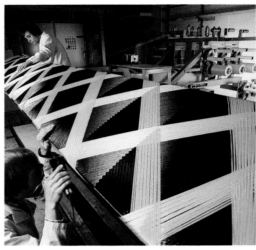

Advances in research and technology evidence themselves here. Above left, like an antenna at 30,000 feet, the Grumman E-2C Hawkeye supports its home-base aircraft carrier with its ability to "see" nearly 300 miles. Above right, inspectors at Sikorsky Aircraft check a composite material made up of Kevlar and graphite fibres bound by epoxy. Left, computerized graphics flash on a transparent display that allows the pilot to monitor weapons systems, radar, and flight orientation without shifting attention.

that many of the computerized missile systems that had been developed were just too complex for pilots to handle under intense combat conditions, and that conventional bombs, destructive as they were, had little effect on a country that had few definable targets to destroy.

The National Aeronautics and Space Administration calls technical advancements from military and space technology "spinoffs." Many such spinoffs have enriched commercial aviation since the sixties. Today, onboard and ground-based computers provide pilots with better information about weather conditions and more accurate navigation. Another important spinoff is in the use of composite materials in airplane construction. Many modern aircraft are now constructed of lightweight combinations of synthetic materials in addition to metal. For commercial airliners such as the wide-body Lockheed L1011, these new "composite" materials reduce weight, save fuel, and so reduce operating costs for the airlines. The airline industry maintains strict standards for the manufacture and construction of these composites, which can include ingredients such as epoxy and graphite.

Though high costs and sophisticated technology mean that not all modern aviation research results in the production of new aircraft, research and testing do not often go to waste. Just as the early aviators learned from their mistakes, modern aerodynamic researchers learn from their experiments, even though it is impossible to put every good idea into production. However, modern experimenters are able, through the use of computers, to carefully preserve and store all kinds of data compiled from their experiments.

In the mid-sixties, the time was right for something new in commercial aviation. First, wide-body jets such as the 747 and the DC-10 were introduced, but the greatest change in commercial aircraft came with supersonic transports, or SSTs. Many people felt that supersonic aircraft could be very valuable in commercial aviation. Perhaps the most significant, albeit limited, contribution to this field was, and still is, the Concorde.

The product of a joint effort by British and French manufacturers, the Concorde travels at Mach 2. Aerodynamically very advanced, the Concorde's hinged nose stays down during ground operations and takeoff, giving the pilot a clear view. In supersonic flight, the nose swings upward to reduce drag. For a number of reasons, primarily economic, the Concorde (or any other supersonic transport) never made great inroads in the field of commercial aviation and only sixteen were ever produced. Fuel costs rose dramatically in the seventies, and most airlines found supersonic transport just too expensive to support. However the Concorde *has* gained a reputation as an elegant and expensive way to fly, and has enlisted a loyal clientele among wealthy and business travelers. Although the promise of supersonic transports constituting the wave of the future did not turn out to be entirely true, a supersonic transport modified to run on new, alternate fuels may still find a place in commercial air travel.

Another revolution that came out of the

technology of the nineteen fifties and sixties was the business-jet aircraft. Before, large corporations had relied on twin-engine aircraft: the Cessna 310, the Aero Commander, or the famous Beech 18. Yet most executives who traveled by air flew by commercial airliners, not company-owned private aircraft. Even the executives at the Boeing aircraft corporation didn't have private planes. They simply weren't speedy or economical enough to operate on a regular basis.

Then, in 1959, the Grumman corporation produced the Gulfstream I. This twin-turboprop masterpiece made executive travel not only comfortable and convenient, but economical as well. Though the first all-jet small craft was introduced by Lockheed in 1957, it wasn't until 1964 that a man named William Lear created the truly outstanding craft in the small-jet field: the Learjet.

The Learjet was based in part on the design of a Swiss fighter plane that had never gone into production. Lear took the Swiss design, modified it, and produced a tiny, highly efficient craft capable of speeds of more than 500 miles per hour. The Learjet had only six seats and was so small that passengers couldn't possibly stand upright in the aisle. Nevertheless, the Learjet took the business world by storm, and "Learjet" became synonymous with business travel all over the world. Today, small jets carry more business and corporate travelers than scheduled commercial flights!

While commercial, military, and even private aircraft moved ahead with startling leaps in design and support technology, the helicop-

ter, too, was undergoing quiet but major improvements. The jet engine proved a great breakthrough in vertical flight. It enabled designers to create the huge, highly efficient choppers that were deployed over Vietnam: the Sikorsky HH-53s or Jolly Green Giants, as they were called by the armed forces. Another innovation in helicopters to come out of the Vietnam conflict was the attack helicopter, most particularly the Bell HueyCobra, a chopper that began a new trend in army support aviation all over the world.

Further improvements in helicopters are just beginning to appear on the horizon. For many years, research has been seeking solutions to the problems of how high-speed horizontal flight can be achieved by vertical-takeoff aircraft. New designs are combining elements of the helicopter with elements of

FEBRUARY 1951   35 CENTS

POPULAR
MECHANICS
MAGAZINE
WRITTEN SO YOU CAN UNDERSTAND IT

See page 118

The current "home-built" movement is perhaps not surprising when, as suggested by this Popular Mechanics *cover from 1951, the idea of owning and garaging one's own aircraft has been around for awhile.*

fixed-wing aircraft. The most successful of these to date, the Bell XV-15, can tilt its rotors and fly like an airplane after a vertical takeoff. The tilt-rotor application may find a future in city-to-city transport, as well as in police work, traffic surveillance, forestry, and other civic uses.

Another smaller, and perhaps quieter, aspect of the current revolution in aviation is in the home-built movement. In many ways, sophistication and skyrocketing costs have taken aviation out of the hands of small companies and designers. Yet a great deal of innovation and expertise is being focused on private and recreational aircraft—ultralight planes, helicopters, and amphibians have all appeared in profusion.

In their own homes, people by the thousands are turning out airplanes of all descriptions, using both conventional and radically new design and construction techniques.

This new surge of enthusiasm makes one thing very clear about the state of modern aviation: No matter what the rising costs of technology, regardless of industry and government regulation, people who love aviation continue to find new, exciting, and innovative ways to fly. And what is more, they have fun doing it.

Below, a Sikorsky X-wing research aircraft takes off with a rotor that becomes a fixed wing for fast flight, an advanced concept that may shorten combat and rescue missions in the future.

FLIGHT TO THE FUTURE

The history of aviation is one of the most exciting stories in the world—almost no area of technology has come so far, so fast. From the days of the Wright brothers and Glenn Curtiss, all the way to the era of those hybrids of air-and-space technology, the *Columbia* and *Challenger* space shuttles, aviation has been filled with miracles of invention and innovation, with brave and dashing heroes, and perhaps most important, with visions of the future.

Today, the visions continue. Flying enthusiasts now have more knowledge and technology at their disposal than ever before, and they are applying that knowledge in the creation of exciting new aircraft. The entire history of aviation is at their disposal, and that history keeps showing up in unexpected ways. Some new privately designed aircraft, for example, have much of the look and feel of the classic planes of the past. Wonderful to look at and fun to fly, many of these planes combine the best of the old glamour and dash of aviation with the best of its new technology—efficient engines and navigation equipment, for example.

As some people did in the days following World War II, many now believe that inexpensive, easy-to-handle private aircraft really constitute aviation's brightest prospects. They look forward to the days when low-cost, individually owned aircraft will be available to everybody. These new planes will be no more difficult to operate than an automobile or even

During nine grueling days between December 14 and 23, 1986, the world watched excitedly as Richard G. Rutan and Jeana Yeager flew Voyager, *left, around the world without stopping or refueling. Designed by Rutan's brother, Burt, the aircraft is built of composite materials, has a wingspan of 111 feet, and weighs 2,680 pounds empty.*

Entirely powered by electricity from solar cells, the Gossamer Penguin *takes off with Paul MacCready's thirteen-year-old son Marshall as the pilot. The craft is a three-quarter scale version of the* Gossamer Albatross—*the first human-powered aircraft to cross the English Channel.*

a bicycle. Advances in computer technology alone indicate what is well within our reach. Far from being an impossible dream, such planes could be made available within only a few years' time.

As an example, try to imagine a small twin-engine aircraft, with no more than a 25-foot wingspan. And then imagine this aircraft equipped with special computerized sensors that would give it automatic stability and control. A plane of this kind would be so "forgiving" in flight that anyone with a minimum of training would be able to take to the skies. Assume that such a plane could be mass manufactured of lightweight, composite materials designed to act as a cushion in the event of collision, and you have what mankind has always yearned for—a personal set of wings, a

"Safebird." Such an aircraft is not here yet, but it is possible.

Many scientists and experimenters are concentrating on the development of just such aircraft. Recently, the work of California designer Paul MacCready has captured the imagination of flight buffs the world over. His man-powered aircraft, including the prize-winning *Gossamer Albatross*, are beautiful and efficient vehicles. The *Gossamer Albatross* was able to bridge such famous obstacles as the English Channel, long a testing place for flight improvements.

MacCready believes that of all the light aircraft available today, the sailplane is the single type of aircraft to make use of the newest in modern flight technology. Built of epoxy and carbon and glass fiber composites, many of

these sailplanes, especially those of European design, have attained a high level of performance and include onboard computers for flight control.

Meanwhile, other experiments also flourish. The *Voyager*, designed by Burt Rutan, drew worldwide acclaim as it completed a nine-day, round-the-world flight on a single tank of fuel. Copiloted by the designer's brother, Richard, and Jeana Yeager, the *Voyager* has a wingspan of 111 feet and is built of highly advanced composite materials. Empty, the graceful craft weighs only 2,680 pounds; full of fuel, almost 12,000 pounds.

Scientists at the Massachusetts Institute of Technology are working on a 100-foot-wingspan, man-powered craft. With a gross weight of less than 70 pounds, this aircraft is being designed to recreate the mythic flight of Icarus and Daedalus, a father and son who supposedly made wings of wax and attempted to fly from the island of Crete to the mainland of Greece, a distance of more than ninety miles.

In addition, some experimenters, like Paul MacCready, are exploring the possibilities of aircraft that draw their energy from sunlight and convert it directly into propulsion. Others concentrate on developing new support technology: computers that can take data from a dozen different sources and integrate it into control outputs that maintain equilibrium in flight. NASA and the military also continue research on the push into space, with preliminary plans for highly advanced space shuttles and even a National Space Plane, a futuristic craft that will accomplish worldwide travel not in the earth's atmosphere, but in space. Too, many dream of the day when such craft will travel to established space stations, shuttling scientists and specialists back and forth throughout the solar system.

Plans for the future of aviation lie in many different directions. Some believe the next great leap forward will come in the creation of private, everyday personal aircraft that will make a pilot's license as commonplace as a driver's license. Others are convinced the next big leap will be into space, with vehicles so advanced that the world can begin the exploration and even colonization of other planets. Still others believe that the future of aviation lies in learning to use what we have to solve problems: the creation of inexpensive, high-energy fuels, for example, that would make ad-

Today's hang glider emulates the birds who first inspired man's quest for flight, though its "wings" are made of cloth and aluminum. Overleaf: right side up or upside down, the wing-walking team of Earl and Paula Cherry thrills crowds at modern airshows with their high-flying stunts.

vancements like supersonic transport practical.

Progress will undoubtedly come in each of these areas. Research in high-energy fuels and solar power is already well under way. Predictions for the future of lightplanes include greater advances in aerodynamics, and the use of autopilot mechanisms and unducted fan jets. There have already been numerous experiments in the development of "convert-iplanes," planes that will convert from air use to road use, allowing the pilot to fly or to drive, as conditions demand. The National Space Plane, now considered a visionary concept, might very well become as common as the old-style freight trains, uniting the world in orbital space travel.

None of these are impossible dreams as we look to the future and the upcoming hundredth anniversary of Wilbur and Orville Wright's first powered flight at Kitty Hawk. By then, perhaps we will have forgotten our differences and begun that worldwide effort to conquer the frontiers of space. By then, perhaps we may have developed the fuels and technology necessary to make our flying machines the best the world has ever seen. In the future, we may fly rather than drive to our schools, supermarkets, and short vacations.

Perhaps the best way to predict the future of flight is to use the same words that Orville Wright used when he was asked to do the same almost a century ago:

"I cannot answer," he said, "except to assure you that it will be spectacular."

INDEX

ACKNOWLEDGMENTS

Alfred Bachmeier, *Chief, Collections Management, Preservation, Restoration, and Storage Division*

Kathleen Brooks-Pazmany, *Research Assistant, National Air and Space Museum*

John C. Burton, *EAA Chief of Public Relations*

Ed Castle, *free-lance photographer*

Paul E. Ceruzzi, *Curator of Science and Technology, National Air and Space Museum*

Edward Chalkley, *Assistant Director for Operations, Preservation, Restoration, and Storage Division*

Ross Chapple, *free-lance photographer*

Rita Cipalla, *Chief, Public Affairs and Museum Services, National Air and Space Museum*

R.E.G. Davies, *Curator, National Air and Space Museum*

Alexis Doster III, *Senior Editor, Smithsonian Books*

Joe Goodwin, *Editor, Smithsonian Books*

Mary Henderson, *Curator of Art, National Air and Space Museum*

Bill Hezlep, *cartographer*

Peter L. Jakab, *Historian, National Air and Space Museum*

Carol James, *Smithsonian Docent*

Brian Kennedy, *Research Editor, Smithsonian Books*

John G. King, *R.R. Donnelley & Sons Company*

George C. Larson, *Editor, Air & Space Magazine*

Susan Lawson, *Museum Technician, Art, National Air and Space Museum*

Russell E. Lee, *Curatorial Assistant, National Air and Space Museum*

Donald S. Lopez, *Deputy Director, National Air and Space Museum*

Mary Ellen McCaffrey, *Production Control Officer, Smithsonian Institution Photo Services*

Mark McCandlish, *artist*

Lester Myers, *Museum Protection Officer, NASM*

A. Nailer, *Librarian, The Royal Aeronautical Society*

Annie Nelson, *Security Aide, NASM*

Stefan Nicolaou, *Musée de l'Air*

Barbara O'Malley, *Smithsonian Docent*

Norberto Parris, *Museum Protection Officer, NASM*

Roberto Pulos, *Mobile Equipment Operator Leader, National Air and Space Museum*

Walter Roderick, *Chief, Production, Operations, Preservation, Restoration, and Storage Division, National Air and Space Museum*

Frances C. Rowsell, *Picture Editor, Smithsonian Books*

Karl S. Schneide, *Curatorial Assistant, National Air and Space Museum*

Caroline Sheen, *free-lance photographer*

Pete Suthard, *Chief, Information Management Division, National Air and Space Museum*

James Trimble, *National Archives*

Robert van der Linden, *Assistant Curator, National Air and Space Museum*

Estelle Washington, *Mobile Equipment Operator Leader, National Air and Space Museum*

Ivory J. Williams, *Museum Protection Officer, NASM*

Lawrence E. Wilson, *Technical Information Specialist, National Air and Space Museum*

PHOTO CREDITS

Front Matter p. 1 NASM/SI; 2–3 NASM/SI; 4–5 Fred J. Maroon; 6–7 Fred J. Maroon

Part 1 From Dream to Reality pp. 8–9 LC; 10 NASM/SI, photo by Ed Castle; 13 NASM/SI; 14 The Bettmann Archive; 15 NASM/SI; 16 NASM/SI; 17 LC; 18–19 NASM/SI; 20 courtesy of Musée de l'Air; 22 NASM/SI; 24–25 NASM/SI; 26 The Bettmann Archive; 28 NASM/SI; 28–29 L'Illustration/SYGMA; 30 NASM/SI; 31 NASM/SI Libraries; 32 *Harriet Quimby, 1911*, Flohri, NASM/SI; 33 NASM/SI, photo by Ross Chapple.

Part 2 Two Wars and Between pp. 34–35 The Bettmann Archive; 35–36 IWM; 36 NASM/SI, photo by Ed Castle; 38, 39 IWM; 40 NA; 41T NASM/SI; 41B Musée de l'Air; 43T IWM; 43B NASM/SI, 44–45 *Aeroplane Fight Over the Verdun Front*, Henri Farré, courtesy USAF Art Collection; 46L NASM/SI, photo by Ed Castle; 46R NA; 47 NA; 48 NASM/SI, photo by Ed Castle; 51 NA; 52–53 NASM/SI, photo by Ross Chapple; 54–55 *Threatening Weather, But the Mail Must Go Through*, Wilma Wethington, 1983, NASM/SI, gift of the artist; 56 NASM/SI; 57T The Bettmann Archive; 57B NASM/SI, photo by Ed Castle; 58 NASM/SI; 59 NASM/SI, photo by Ross Chapple; 61 NASM/SI; 62 Bella Landauer Sheet Music Collection, NASM/SI Libraries; 63 NASM/SI; 65 NASM/SI, photo by Ed Castle; 66–67 *Hughes Racer*, Bruce Burk, NASM/SI, gift of the artist; 68–69 courtesy of Sikorsky Aircraft; 70 NASM/SI; 71 NASM/SI, photo by Ross Chapple. pp. 72–73 NASM/SI & private collections, photo by Ed Castle; 75 NASM/SI; 76–77 Image in Industry, Ltd., photo by Arthur Gibson; 78 *Into the Teeth of the Tiger*, William S. Phillips, © 1984, reprinted by permission of Greenwich Workshop, Inc. CT, on loan to NASM/SI by Donald S. Lopez; 79 *Hans-Ulrich Rudel at Work*, Keith Ferris; 80 NA; 81 LC; 82 *Tora! Tora! Tora!*, Robert McCall, reproduced courtesy of the artist, on loan to NASM/SI, photo by Ed Castle; 83 Franklin D. Roosevelt Library; 84 *Douglas SBD-3*, R.G. Smith, NASM/SI, gift of MPB Corp.; 85 NASM/SI, photo by Ed Castle; 86 AD III, photo by Ed Castle; 87T NASM/SI, USAF Collection; 87B NASM/SI.

Part 3 Jets, Rockets, and Realism pp. 88–89 NASM/SI, photo by Ross Chapple; pp. 90–91 NASM/SI, photo by Ross Chapple; 92–93 Herman J. Kokojan/Black Star; 95 courtesy of Lockheed-California Co.; 96 NASM/SI; 97 NASM/SI; 98T courtesy Rockwell International; 98B *MiG Might*, Mark McCandlish, 1986, donated to San Diego Aerospace Museum, photo by Ed Castle; 99 de Haviland/Air Pilots Assoc.; 100–101 NASM/SI; 102–103 Erik Simonsen; 104–105 George Hall/Woodfin Camp & Assoc.; 106 courtesy Lockheed-California Co.; 108TL Fred J. Maroon; 108TR courtesy Sikorsky Aircraft; 108B Michael Melford/Wheeler Pictures; 110 Image in Industry, Ltd., photo by Arthur Gibson; 111 Robert Ellison/Black Star; 112 Popular Mechanics Magazine; 113 courtesy of Sikorsky Aircraft; 114–115 J.P. Laffont/SYGMA; 116–117 James Sugar/Black Star; 118–119 Erik Simonsen; 120–121 Jim Koepnick/EAA.

FOR FURTHER READING

AMERICAN HERITAGE, EDS. *The American Heritage History of Flight*. American Heritage Publishing Co., 1962.

BILSTEIN, ROGER E. *Flight in America 1900–1983*. Johns Hopkins University Press, 1984.

CHRISTY, JOE. *The Illustrated Handbook of Aviation and Aerospace Facts*. TAB Books, 1984.

CROUCH, TOM D. *The Eagle Aloft: Two Centuries of Ballooning in America*. Smithsonian Institution Press, 1983.

TAYLOR, JOHN, ED. *The Lore of Flight*. Chancellor Press, 1986.